Children of Alcoholics:

Selected Readings

Dear Linda,

Thanks for the difference you make! Celebrate you.

Love,

Jerry

ISBN 0-9645327-0-0
Cover design and book layout: Eric Moore, 1995.
©COPYRIGHT 1995

National Association for Children of Alcoholics (NACoA)
11426 Rockville Pike, Suite 100
Rockville, MD. 20852 301-468-0985 Fax 301-468-0987

TABLE OF CONTENTS

CONTRIBUTING WRITERS

Hoover Adger, Jr., M.D., M.P.H.
Associate Professor of Pediatrics
Johns Hopkins University School of Medicine

Claudia Black, Ph.D., M.S.W.
Past Chair of the National Association for Children of Alcoholics

Stephanie Brown, Ph.D.
Director, The Addictions Institute
Co-Director, The Family Recovery Project--Mental Health
Research Institute

Lewis D. Eigen, Ed.D.
President
Social & Health Services, Ltd.

Jeannette Johnson, Ph.D.
University of Maryland at Baltimore
Department of Psychiatry, Division of Alcohol and Drug Abuse

David McDuff, M.D.
University of Maryland at Baltimore
Department of Psychiatry, Division of Alcohol and Drug Abuse

Jerry Moe, M.A.
Children's Program Director at Sierra Tucson, Tucson, AZ

Ellen Morehouse, ACSW, NCAC II
Executive Director
Student Assistance Services Corp.

Jon Rolf, Ph.D.
Kansas State University
Office of Community Health

David W. Rowden, Ph.D.
Director
National Clearinghouse for Alcohol and Drug Information

Stuart Tiegel, L.C.S.W.
University of Maryland at Baltimore
Department of Psychiatry, Division of Alcohol and Drug Abuse

Steven J. Wolin, M.D.
George Washington University Medical School
Project Resilience

Sybil Wolin, Ph.D.
Project Resilience

FOREWORD

You have picked up this book because you care about children of alcoholics, just as we do. One person's addiction has a negative effect on everyone in the family, but the most powerful impact is on the young and vulnerable. Working together, in all our walks of life, we can make a difference for those children.

The National Association for Children of Alcoholics is proud to publish this monograph, which represents a variety of perspectives and professional experience. The contributing writers are among the most distinguished clinicians and researchers in the family addiction field, which needs to bring together impeccable research *and* intuitive clinical experience. We believe the following articles will be useful to you, whether your interest in the subject is personal or professional.

Stephanie Abbott
Editor

Children of Alcoholics: The Role of the Primary Care Physican

Hoover Adger, Jr., M.D., M.P.H.

There are an estimated 28.6 million Americans who are children of alcoholics (COAs), nearly 7 million of them are under the age of 18. Of the under-18 group, nearly 3 million will develop alcoholism, other drug problems, and/or other serious coping problems. Many of these children are exposed to chaotic family environments which lack consistency, stability or emotional support. Some of these children may be traumatized by accidental injury resulting from parental drinking or drug use, verbal abuse or physical abuse. Poor communication, permissiveness, undersocialization, neglect and violence, all potentially devastating, are common in children who live in alcoholic families.[1,2,3]

The cycle is frequently repeated. Approximately half of COAs will marry alcoholics; thus, there is a high likelihood of recreating the same kinds of highly stressful and unhealthy families in which they grew up.

Children of alcoholics are at increased risk because of genetic and/or environmental factors.[4,5] Children living with alcoholics often develop unhealthy living patterns. They may not learn to trust themselves or others, how to handle uncomfortable feelings, or how to build positive relationships. COAs who lack these skills are also at higher risk for school failure, depression, increased anxiety, as well as trouble with alcohol and other drugs.[6,7]

While genetic predisposition can't be changed, unhealthy living patterns can be countered by consistent caring by others. COAs can learn to trust, handle their feelings in healthy ways, and build positive, nurturing relationships. Health care professionals can help COAs understand their risks and learn better social and coping skills.

Impact of Alcoholism on the Family

Families often tend to act in patterned and predictable ways when one member of the family is affected by alcoholism. Over time, affected families move away from the supportive relationships that characterize healthy families and move toward increasingly dysfunctional states. Denial, secretiveness, lack of trust and honesty, and suppression of feelings are patterns which are often observed.

Denial can be a powerful but maladaptive defense and may prevent individuals from recognizing the root cause of a deteriorating family relationship. Hence, actions that are obvious indicators of problems related to alcohol use may become accepted as everyday behavior by the family. The family denial may be even stronger than that of the affected individual and may be related to the amount of stigmatization felt by family members. Denial may be so pervasive that, even when an alcohol problem is suspected, affected family members may unconsciously mislead health practitioners into pursuing other causes for stress in the family.[8] Because of the power of denial, the illness may progress notably and health practitioners, at times, may become frustrated in their attempts to confirm a suspected diagnosis. The importance of recognizing denial is underscored by the fact that it is not uncommon for a spouse or child in the family to feel that they are the cause of the deteriorating family relationship. Hence, historical information and attribution may be markedly distorted.

Once family members recognize that a parent, child or spouse has alcoholism, they may attempt to adapt in a number of ways to insure the integrity of the family unit. They may not discuss the problem among themselves or with others outside of the family. Even young children learn not to share painful and distressing observations; instead, family members hide the problem and their reactions from each other. A spouse who is physically abused by the affected individual may tell the children that they fell. The drinking is not mentioned nor confirmed, and the family secret grows.

The isolation that develops around the family is both social and emotional. Children stop inviting friends over because of the unpredictability of the alcoholic's behavior. A spouse may refuse social invitations or make excuses for the alcoholic's absence from work. These behavior patterns - denial, secretiveness, lack of honesty, and suppression of feelings - are amazingly similar and parallel to those of the alcoholic. At times, the boundaries around families can become rigid and impermeable with a restricted flow of information passing into and out of the family. In such situations, normal needs may be gratified in abnormal ways. For example, the incidence of sexual abuse is reportedly high in substance abusing families. Often the victim will suffer in silence and will not reveal the abuse for many years.

As the family becomes increasingly preoccupied with the alcoholic's drinking, there are attempts to reorganize, and various adaptive roles may be taken on. Sharon Wegscheider described stereotypic roles in the alcoholic family and dysfunctional families in general, which have become popularized in the lay literature - the alcoholic, the enabler, the scapegoat, the lost child, and the mascot. The alcoholic is the central character in the family's drama. The enabler, frequently the spouse, takes control of the family and protects the affected person from facing the consequences of his/her behavior by assuming the alcoholic's responsibilities and by shielding his/her actions from others. While this family member is usually perceived as extremely responsible and strong-willed, they can have a number of negative feelings inside. Frustration, anxiety and stress related symptoms are an understandable corollary of enabling behaviors. The hero is often a high achiever and brings pride to the family by being successful at school or work. While portraying an image of self confidence and success, the hero may feel inadequate and experience the same stress related symptoms as the enabler. The scapegoat diverts attention away from the alcoholic by acting out his/her anger. The scapegoat is considered to be at high risk for addiction because of his/her association with risk taking activities and peers and may be progressively involved in self-injurious and delinquent behaviors. The lost child, often characterized as quiet and shy, withdraws from the family and social activities to escape the problem. The mascot is the one who seeks attention for being cute or funny, demonstrates immature behavior, and may have difficulty learning in school. While laughing on the outside, he/she may be quite sad on the inside.

For the physician, the importance of understanding these roles lies not only in the insight it provides about the dynamics of the alcoholic's family, but it may assist the physician in identifying health problems related to maladaptive behaviors.[9] Although the roles are stereotypical, patients may describe themselves in these terms. Hence, it may be supportive for the patient if the physician understands. An appreciation of family dynamics may put the physician in a better position to assist patients in learning more functional coping strategies.

Often, the behavior exhibited by COAs brings them to professional attention before alcoholism is diagnosed in a parent or other family member. The impact of an alcoholic parent on the child can be devastating. The younger a child is when drinking begins, the more serious is its impact on the child's subsequent adult life.[8] When family alcohol and other drug abuse is untreated, children often carry the family rules and role-related behaviors into adulthood.

While heavy bias exists in studies emphasizing the illness or damage model in children of alcoholics, the majority of children in an alcoholic family become healthy, well-adjusted adults. It appears that there are protective mechanisms that enable many COAs to grow into well functioning adults. Children of alcoholics who do not develop serious coping problems are distinguished from their peers by more attention from their primary caretaker early in life and absence of prolonged separations. These resilient children appear to have more affectionate temperaments in childhood, have at least average intelligence, possess adequate communication skills, maintain a positive self-image, and have a more internalized locus of control.[10]

Steinglass and colleagues have found that families differ in their responses to the effects of alcoholism. Their research has highlighted that the family's rituals, priorities and behavioral styles and their uses of resources and energy are altered by alcoholism. Many families are successful at maintaining their primary tasks and are not identified as problematic. In families where the alterations are the greatest, learned behaviors are passed on to the next generation. When the family is able to resist the full effects of the disease, the children do not necessarily recreate the same kinds of highly stressful and unhealthy families in which they grew up.[11,12]

Physicians who understand these behaviors and associated symptoms can be helpful in uncovering the problem of alcoholism, in explaining to the family how they may be affected by the problem, and by providing valuable assistance to the family and the problem drinker.

Intervention and Treatment

Understanding the many ways in which alcohol and other drug use and abuse affects families can be helpful in formulating a plan for intervention and treatment. The family can be instrumental in initiating treatment. Even when the person with problem drinking is highly resistent or unwilling to participate in treatment, the clinician may still have a highly motivated patient(s); i.e., the family.

The first step in intervention and treatment is identification. A number of instruments have been developed to screen large populations at risk. Two common examples are the CAGE and CAST (Children of Alcoholics Screening Test). The CAGE is a simple 4 question screening tool which has been used as a measure of problem drinking in adults and can easily be incorporated into the medical history. A simple modification of the CAGE screening questions, the "Family CAGE," can be administered to each family member. The Children of Alcoholics Screening Test, in contrast, measures the impact of a parent's drinking on the child. Screening and referral can be an important role for the primary care provider and should be performed as a routine part of the health visit.[13,14,9] The complexity and diversity of problems encountered in many children of alcoholics require early and comprehensive intervention. The primary care provider needs to be acquainted with the vast array of health professionals in the community who can be enlisted to assist in the evaluation, assessment and treatment of affected families. Common intervention strategies, which include delivering developmentally and age appropriate education, connecting patients with social support networks, offering training in skill development and addressing the socio-emotional needs of affected individuals, should be familiar to health practitioners.

Conclusion

Primary care providers encounter large numbers of patients who are affected by alcoholism in the family. Pediatricians and other primary health care providers are in an ideal position to identify early alcohol and other drug related problems in children, adolescents and families. While it is easiest to identify alcohol related effects in those patients who are most severely affected, the challenge before health care providers is to identify individuals early in their involvement and to intervene in a very timely and meaningful manner. Appreciating the magnitude of the problem, the nature of the disease, and the role of the health provider in the prevention, intervention and treatment of the problem are vital.

References

1. *Alcoholism tends to run in families. DHHS publication No. (ADM) 92-1914, 1992.*

2. *Russell M, Henderson C, and Blume SB. Children of Alcoholics: A Review of the Literature. New York, NY: Children of Alcoholics Foundation, 1985.*

3. *National Institute on Alcohol Abuse and Alcoholism. Eighth Special Report to the U.S. Congress on Alcohol and Health. NIH Publ. No. 94-3699. Bethesda, MD: National Institutes of Health, 1993.*

4. *Begleiter H, Porjesz B, Bihari B, Kissin B. Event-related brain potentials in boys at risk for alcoholism. Science 227:1493-1496, 1984.*

5. *Anthenelli RM, Schuckit MA. Genetic studies of alcoholism. Int J Addict 25:81-94, 1990.*

6. *Wegscheider S. Another Chance. Palo Alto, Science and Behavior Books, Inc, 1981.*

7. *Black C. It Will Never Happen to Me. Denver, Medical Administration Company, 1982.*

8. *Estes N, Heinemann M (eds). Alcoholism, Development, Consequences, and Interventions, ed 2. St. Louis, CV Mosby Co, 1982.*

9. Duggan AK, Adger H, McDonald EM, et al. Detection of Alcoholism in children and their families. *Am J Dis Child*, 145:613-7, 1991.

10. Werner EE. Resilient Offspring of Alcoholics: A Longitudinal Study from Birth to Age 18. *Journal of Studies on Alcohol*, 47:34-40, 1986

11. Steinglass P, Bennett LA, Wolin SJ, Reis D. *The Alcoholic Family*. Basic Books, Inc., New York, 1987.

12. Wolin SJ, Bennett LA, Noonan DL, Teitelbaum MA. Disrupted family rituals: a factor in the intergenerational transmission of alcoholism. *Journal of Studies on Alcohol*, 41: 199-214, 1980.

13. Graham AV. Family Issues in Substance Abuse. Project SAEFP, Society of Teachers of Family Medicine, DHHS No. 240-89-0038, 1990.

14. MacDonald DI, Blume SB. Children of Alcoholics. *AJDC*, 140: 750, 1986.

You Can't Go Forward Without Finishing the Past
Healing the Pain of Abandonment, Fear, and Shame

Claudia Black, Ph.D., M.S.W.

"In this dream I was stationed underground, in the grave....This was my company, my life, my mission—to watch over the bones. And then slowly... I walked away and climbed out of the grave, into the sun and the wide expanse of the world....I turned one last time to say good-bye. The vigil of the bones was over."

—John, Adult Child of an Alcoholic,
Quoted by Stephanie Brown, Safe Passages

"To free yourself from the past you must break the rules of silence and compliance."

— Claudia Black, It's Never Too Late to
Have a Happy Childhood

When children are raised with chronic loss, without the psychological or physical protection they need, and certainly deserve, it is most natural for them to internalize fear. Not having the necessary psychological or physical protection equals abandonment. And, living with repeated abandonment experiences creates shame. Shame arises from the painful message implied in abandonment: "You are not important. You are not of value." Both the pain of the past, as yet unresolved, and pain in the present, created by past-driven behaviors, fuel our fear of abandonment and shame. This is the pain from which we need to heal.

PAIN FROM THE PAST

Physical Abandonment

For some children abandonment is primarily physical. Physical abandonment occurs when parents do not provide the physical conditions necessary for thriving, such as:
- lack of appropriate supervision.
- inadequate nutrition and meals provided.

There was a book titled *Potato Chips for Breakfast*, and a talk by educator and lecturer Dan Barmettle called "Macaroni at Midnight"; these titles so poignantly reflect the poor eating habits of children in some families.

- inadequate clothing, housing, heat, or shelter.
- physical and/or sexual abuse.

As children, we are totally dependent on our caretakers to provide safety in our environment. When they do not, we grow up believing that the world is an unsafe place, that people are not to be trusted, and that we do not deserve positive attention and adequate care.

Emotional Abandonment

Emotional abandonment occurs when parents do not provide the emotional conditions and emotional environment necessary to growing up freely, in accordance with the child's own nature.

Because more people experience emotional abandonment than physical abandonment and because it is a more subtle dynamic, the following abandonment experiences may be helpful to understanding emotional abandonment.

- Children have to hide a part of their beings in order to be accepted. Many children experience rejection when they make mistakes and are less than perfect, or when they express needs, show feelings, or when they have successes.

All of these experiences could be met by disapproval, rejection, or even punishment.

- Children cannot live up to the expectations of their parents. These expectations are often unrealistic and not age-appropriate.
- Children are held responsible for other people's behavior. They may be consistently blamed for the actions and feelings of their parents.
- Disapproval is shown toward children that is aimed at their entire beings or identity rather than a particular behavior. Who the child is, is not separated out from what the child does.

Abandonment and Boundaries

Many times our abandonment issues are fused with distorted, confused, or undefined personal boundaries. We experience abandonment when parents have a distorted sense of boundaries, both their boundaries and ours.

When parents do not view us as separate beings with distinct boundaries and find value in us as such, we will experience abandonment. They want us to like what they like, dress like they dress, and feel as they do. This is particularly painful during our teenage years when it is only normal in our development to seek out behaviors different from the parent's as a part of the process of developing and knowing our own self. While this teenage/parent struggle is common to many, some parents cannot recognize this as part of the adolescent stage, but see it as a personal affront to their image, their own source of worth. If we in any way express differences from our parents, or make different choices than they would, we know we run the risk of rejection.

When parents expect us to be extensions of themselves, fulfilling their dreams, we will feel abandoned. How many of us went to the school our father wanted to go to, but wasn't able to? How many entered into careers that our parents chose for us? How many of us married who we did, when we did because that was expected or desired by our parents? I offer a caution in that having done what our parents expected, wanted, or demanded does not mean that it was the wrong thing to do. It just so often means that the decision was never totally ours. It is the process that is more painful or possibly wrong, not necessarily the out-come.

Judy told how her mother spoke as if it were simply fact that neither of her daughters were to have children when they reached childbearing age due to the possibility of transmitting a terminal genetic disease. "My mom made it clear that it was not an option. Because that decision seemed based in her wanting to protect us from pain, and to protect a child from having to die, it was hard to want to question this dictate. Mom's motivation was sincere. But I was twenty-nine years old when I realized I had never made my own decision about this. Until then it had been my mother's dictate. I realized I had to sit down and separate my life choices from my mother's pain in having a child who died young. I wrestled with the decision for a few years and ultimately made the decision to not have a child. Today, the decision is mine, not my mother's."

Certainly, many people do exactly what their parents don't want them to do. Often this is a part of their attempt to be able to be a separate person. We don't marry the person our father so liked. We don't go to the college our mother aspired to attend. And often we choose to marry the person they would like the least and simply choose to not attend college at all. Again, it is not the outcome that is the issue, as much as it is the decision-making process. Instead of choosing freely, we make a reactive decision based in anger.

When parents are not willing to take responsibility for their feelings, thoughts, and behaviors, but expect us to take responsibility for them, we will experience abandonment. When parents hold children responsible for what should be their responsibility, they are expecting something impossible for a child. In effect, they are telling children that they have more power than in fact they have, setting them up to experience futility and inadequacy.

When parents' self-esteem is derived through our behavior, their needs override ours, and so once again, we feel abandoned. Henri still feels pain when he talks about how his father publicly gloated over Henri's accomplishments. "Some people told me I should be grateful that my dad even noticed what I was involved in. But there was as always something missing about his being proud of me. When I was growing up, I did well in school, I was a very good athlete. I was a student leader and often had my picture in the local paper. My dad came to my events, boasting about me in a way that never seemed real. His boasting was so grand and his need for people to know it was his son was so strong. Yet there was this total lack of interest in me when I was home. When I got home from the ball games, he would already be in bed. He never boasted to me. He never once congratulated me or patted me on the back."

As readers, we can each interpret Henri's situation differently. What is important to note is that Henri did not get the validation he needed to feel special, of value, and important to his father. What he believed was that his value to his father was in how he could make his father look to his father's peers.

When children are treated as peers with no parent/child distinction, they will feel abandoned by their parents. Many times parents develop relationships with their children in which they are their friends, their peers, their equals. In doing so, they share information that is not age-appropriate for a child. Inappropriate information often creates a sense of burden, or even guilt for children, and that is not fair. To tell a ten-year-old daughter that her father has had an affair cannot offer the daughter any security. The mother may need to talk about it, but that needs to be with someone who has the adult resources to be able to offer appropriate support or feedback. To share with an eight-year-old son the fears related to a situation at work only makes the child feel that his parent needs support and is too vulnerable to be available as a source of protection.

Abandonment plus distorted boundaries at a time when children are developing their sense of worth is the foundation to the belief in their own inadequacy, and the central cause of their shame.   When parents are disrespectful of their children's boundaries and violate them, the message given is that they don't value a child as a person. That message becomes internalized as "I am not of value. I am not worthy." When parents don't acknowledge children's boundaries, the message they give is "You are here to meet my needs," and/or "I am more important than you," and/or "It is not okay to be your own person with individual feelings, desires, or needs." The message also implies that the children have to give up themselves to be available to another. This internalizes to the belief, "I am bad for having different, or separate needs, wants, and feelings." "I, in my uniqueness, am not of value." When children experience chronic abandonment with distorted boundaries, they live in fear and doubt about their worth.

The greater the clarity a child has around boundaries, understanding who is responsible for what, and the greater a child's self-esteem, the more likely a child will be able to reject, rather than internalize, shameful behaviors and messages. The following is an example of a young person, Sandi, who, in spite of the fact that she was raised in an alcoholic family, experienced some stability in her early years. As a result, she developed a sense of self and self-esteem which helped her ward off shame. "Up until I was about eight, home seemed okay. I felt valued, life was fun. Then as if it was overnight, my dad was always angry. My mom was preoccupied and distant or very sad. It was as if neither of our parents had any time for us. Looking back now I realized that something was happening. I just couldn't figure it out. No one was talking about what was wrong. Life just became more frightening. I tried not to get in the way. I took care of my brother and sister. I tried to do things to make my dad and mom happy. Nothing I did really made a difference."

Because Sandi had experienced security and safety in her very early years though, she developed a sense of self-worth and a degree of autonomy that helped prevent her from taking on shame. One night when she was sixteen and cheerleading at a basketball game, her father showed up so drunk he could hardly walk on his own and created a scene that nearly incited a racial riot. With his arms thrown over her shoulders and her pom poms tucked under her arms, Sandi was leading her drunk father out of the gym when he began to scream racial slurs at a group of African- American teenagers. "He said things I never heard him or any one else say," Sandi said. "He said things I never knew he thought. Thank heaven this group of kids couldn't reach us. It was all I could do to get him out of the gym. Everyone was screaming and jeering. Well, I got him into his friend's car and off they went. I didn't know why my dad acted like he did — I was so angry at him."

Sandi had the ability to be angry because she had not previously internalized shame and therefore could clearly differentiate who was responsible for what. She had healthy boundary distinction. She knew what took place in the gym was about her father, not her. Because she did not take this incident as a statement about her worth or value, she was also able to access other feelings. With shame, we lose the ability to identify our feelings and we are more likely to reinstate the Don't Talk rule. Sandi said she was angry, and then became sad. She could talk about her fear. While this scene was certainly an act of abandonment by her father, she nonetheless had an emotional boundary that protected her self-worth and her autonomy.

Sandi's ability to maintain a healthy emotional boundary ("My father's behavior does not determine who I am."), which prevented her from feeling shamed and personally diminished by her father's behavior, requires the same kind of skills necessary to ward off shame in a less public situation.   Linda was born into an already hectic, frightened family. Her first memories were of hiding behind a table in the kitchen, trying not to be noticed, while listening to her parents arguing and thinking to herself, "Just don't let them see me." She spent most of her life trying to be invisible. "In my family there was a lot of arguing, unhappiness, and a lot of moving from place to place. I was the youngest of four and an unplanned pregnancy. My mother let me know right away she was content with three babies, not four. I felt I came out of the shoot needing a protective shield, trying to ward off the hurtful words, the painful glares. I was always in their way. Yet I worked so hard not to be. My very existence seemed like such a thorn." When childhood is like Linda's, spent on survival, there is little energy left to develop a separate sense of self, an autonomous self. Linda was chronically abandoned, subject to emotional boundary abuse, and as a result, experienced and internalized shame.

When we are, in essence, abandoned by our caretakers, we will not perceive that they were bad people or what they did to us was bad. Children cannot reject bad parents because parents are needed so desperately. Children always feel that a bad object is better than no object at all. Instead, they will internalize that they are bad themselves. In other words, children take the burden of badness on themselves.   In doing this, they purge their caretakers of badness, which reinforces a sense of security. It is well recognized that mistreated children who cope with intolerable environments are, in fact, very apt to project goodness onto their parents and badness onto themselves. In effect, outer safety is purchased at the price of inner security.

Abandonment, plus distorted or undefined boundaries as you are developing your worth and identity, creates shame and fear. This truth bears repeating because it defines the root of our pain. What we must understand now is that our abandonment experiences and boundary violations were in no way indictments of our innate goodness and value. Instead, they revealed the flawed thinking, false beliefs, and impaired behaviors of those who hurt us. Still, the wounds were struck deep in our young hearts and minds, and the very real pain can still be felt today. The causes of our emotional injury need to be understood and accepted so we can heal. Until we do, the pain will stay with us, becoming a driving force in our adult lives.

PAST-DRIVEN, PRESENT PAIN

In recovery we seek to change the course in our present lives by healing the pain of our past. That means we also must address the pain that results from our past-driven, present-day beliefs and behaviors. As a result of the pain of our past experiences, we adopted false beliefs, i.e., "I can't make a mistake or I will be worthless," or "I have to produce to be of value." We learned defense skills, i.e., to blame others before they blame us. We developed cognitive defense mechanisms, i.e., to deny, minimize, or rationalize. We developed mechanisms to distract us from our pain, i.e., excessive behaviors, or we found ways to literally numb our pain, i.e., food or alcohol and other drugs. All of these are strategies for the preservation of ourselves when our Self is threatened.

Jan said, "I knew my parents loved me. They provided for me. They came to my school events. They told me they loved me. They would hug me. Yet, they would blatantly reject me if I showed feelings of sadness or anger. There was clearly a Don't Talk rule around being emotional unless the feelings were positive. My shame was for having feelings. So while I knew I was valued in one way, I felt very rejected and abandoned in other ways. There was a lot of loss in my family. My dad lost his job and did not find one for four years. My mother had to be hospitalized for unknown reasons twice when I was between nine and eleven. My sister went to live with my grandmother during those times. And we weren't to talk about any of this. I was angry. I was very frightened. I was sad. I wanted to scream so I could be heard, and yet knew I would not be heard and only banished further."

Jan did what most of us do when feeling abandonment and fear— she did her best to be "lovable" so her family would be there for her. Being lovable would be defined by others. For Jan,

16

it meant discounting her own feelings and needs and putting those of others ahead of hers, which in turn meant distancing from herself. Jan learned these defenses and skills as a young girl and now these are the only defenses and skills she knows for protecting herself and relating to others. Paradoxically, Jan's beliefs and behaviors do not protect her now, but actually cause her more pain. Unfortunately, these will continue throughout her adult life until the painful weight of chronically discounting her needs and feelings is so great that she is no longer able to continue as she has. Then she will seek new, different protectors, often harmful ways, such as alcohol or prescription pills. These present-day protections will only perpetuate, and probably escalate, her pain until she turns from the course of protecting from pain to the path of healing her pain.

Most people develop protective strategies when they are young, carrying them into adulthood with slight, age-related differences. For example, as a child you may have used food to medicate your pain, and continue to use food this way as an adult, but now also use alcohol as a medication. Or, as a child, if you used people-pleasing behaviors to get attention from parents, you may also employ this strategy to get attention in the work place.

The mechanisms we develop to reduce our anxiety and fears are defensive protectors. *In no way should we ever be critical of what we needed to do to protect ourselves growing up.* Today, though, we need to recognize when these defenses and protectors are intrusive in our lives, or when they create more harm and pain. The purpose or theme of these strategies has been to lessen the perception or feeling of abandonment; also to compartmentalize or distance ourselves from the incredible fear and sense of powerlessness. The basis for all these attempts is to control or compensate for the pain.

The burden of pain we presently carry and try so hard to control is the combination of unresolved pain from the past *plus* pain from the present. As we know, events and family conditions that caused our past pain cannot be changed, but our response to pain is a choice we are making in the present. And how we choose to respond can change the course of our lives. Our pain, our choice of responses, and the consequences of our choices are summarized on the following chart, "Pain from an Adult's Point of View."

From A Past of Chronic Loss To the Turning Point
Pain from an Adult's Point of View

Unresolved past pain
Chronic loss
Abandonment experiences
Shame, guilt
Sadness, anger

Past-driven present pain
Fear: I will be abandoned again
Shame from past: I was abandoned,
so I am unloveable, unworthy

Shame in present: ashamed of ways
I control pain, fear, shame

Present pain load
Consequence of persistent loss, abandonment; triggered
by current conflict or loss event

CYCLE OF PAIN RESPONSES

Feel Pain and/or	**Control Pain** and/or	**Control Source Pain**
(Emotional response)	(Behavioral response)	(Rational response)
Victim Rage Depression	Addiction Complusion	Perfectionism Procrastination
"I have power/no power over my pain."	"I will numb, reduce, erase my pain."	"I will remove the source of my pain."

TURNING POINT: "I can choose the way I respond to my pain"

Repeat response cycle:
Pain escalates
Response escalates
Shame deepens

CHANGING COURSE:
Recovery process begins
Pain lessens as it heals
Pain control behaviors modify, end

Progressively pain-filled,
self-destructive life

Progressively pain-free,
spiritual life

Causes of past pain cannot be changed.
Responses to pain, both past and present, can change.
Changing responses to pain changes the course of
pain in life.

© *Changing Course,* Claudia Black

18

In the next pages, we'll discuss how people respond to pain so we will be able to understand the choices we can make.

ATTEMPTS TO CONTROL OUR PAIN

Whether or not we understood the source of our pain in our early lives, we felt it. We were anxious, fearful, saddened, or angry. To live with a high degree of emotional pain was so unbearable for most of us that we sought ways to control the pain to defend against it. Ironically and unfortunately, as we have now seen, these ways created their own pain.

As adults still trying to control our pain, we have sought ways to create a sense of control or power, to compensate for the overwhelming experience of powerlessness. We have attempted to control the pain and/or to control the sources of pain. We have tried to be in control to protect ourselves from further exposure, so that our vulnerability would not be visible. We have tried to be in control so that no one would ever shame us again and so that we would not have to feel our pain.

We feel our pain. We medicate our pain. We rationalize our pain. These are all responses to the pain we have felt for so long. Then we have responded to our feeling powerless over the pain, or powerless to be able to impact our own lives in a way that creates a difference.

We first respond to pain on an emotional level, most commonly in terms of victimization, rage, and depression. Then, in an attempt to control the pain, we may respond with behaviors that try to medicate it with alcohol, drugs, foods, or compulsive behaviors. Last, we may respond on a rational level, thinking we can avoid the pain if we don't do anything to cause it. Perfectionism and procrastination are two cognitive attempts to control pain by avoiding it.

EMOTIONAL RESPONSES TO PAIN

Victimization As A Response To Pain

Chronic victimization, that is, chronically assuming the role of the victim, is the result when we accept and operate on the shameful

19

messages that we internalized as a result of the abandonment. It is a combination of not believing in our own worth, and not developing the skills that go with a belief in our worthiness, such as setting limits. When we have internalized beliefs, such as "I am not worthy," "I am not of value," "Other people are more important than I," or "Other people are more worthy," then it is difficult to set limits. We don't believe we have the right to set limits. We do not know how to say no. Those of us who are victims struggle with appropriate boundaries. We are most apt not to have boundaries or boundaries that are easily permeable.

Victims have learned not to trust their own perceptions, believing that another person's perception is accurate instead of theirs. They always give others the benefit of the doubt and are willing to respond to the structure others set. Victims are not apt to question. After all, they believe "Who am I to question?"

Not believing in their own worth, victims often fail to realize they even have needs and, as a result, do not take care of themselves. They operate from a position of fear, unable to access any anger or indignation that comes with being hurt, or disappointed, or even abused. When asked what they need or want, victims often do not know.

While the development of the victim response is enveloped by the deepest belief in personal powerlessness, it is clearly a response to the intense emotional pain in one's life. It not only is an outcome of helplessness, it is also a kind of defense in that victims believe they may not have as much pain if they give in to, or abdicate, their autonomy to another.

Victims have developed a high tolerance for pain and for inappropriate behavior. They have become emotionally separated from themselves by becoming highly skilled at rationalizing, minimizing, and often flatly denying the events and emotions in their lives. They are not as readily able to identify others' behavior that has hurt them because that would, in their perception, create a greater feeling of helplessness or invite more trouble.

Some victims stay in isolation. Those who choose to stay more visible often play a victim/martyr situation: "Look at how I am victimized! Aren't they terrible for doing this to me! I will just have to endure." Being victim becomes part of a cycle. Victims already feel bad about themselves as a result of being abandoned and/or used and abused. Then they don't act in a way that provides safety and security for themselves, leading to greater abandonment, use or abuse.

Typically, the greater a person's shame, the more likely he or she will invite someone else with tremendous shame into their lives. Very often, for the victim, this other person is someone who appears to have the ability to take charge, make things happen, someone who feels strength by association with the victim's vulnerability. Depending on the specific history of the two people involved, that attraction often leads to the dominant one battering the victim, either emotionally or physically.

Almost inevitably, victims have great difficulty protecting themselves in the context of intimate relationships. For example, a woman may have such a desperate longing for nurturance and care that it makes it difficult for her to establish safe and appropriate boundaries with others. Her tendency to denigrate herself and to idealize those to whom she becomes attached further clouds her judgment. In this case, her empathic attunement to the wishes of others and her automatic, often unconscious habits of obedience also make her vulnerable to anyone in a position of power or authority. Her defensive style makes it difficult for her to form conscious and accurate assessments of danger.

For all of the reasons noted above, whether male or female, the shameful person is at great risk of repeated victimization.

Rage As Response To Pain

Rage is the holding tank for accumulated fears, angers, humiliations, and shame. It is an honest response to no longer wanting to endure the pain. Emotionally, rage is an attempt to be heard, seen, and valued when people are most desperate and lacking in other resources. For some people rage becomes integrated into their lifestyle. Growing up, they found anger to be the one safe feeling for them to express, so all their other vulnerabilities were masked with anger. Many people who are rageful don't show any sign of emotions, keeping a tight lid on all of their feelings until something triggers an eruption. There may not be signs of any feeling, and suddenly their rage is in someone else's face, a scathing memo at work; an outburst of criticism at service providers, i.e., waiters, gas station attendants, etc.; a lack of tolerance for any disagreement in a discussion, followed by a theatrical exit, or a lashing out verbally or physically.

While people with chronic rage do exist, they are not tolerated in most neighborhoods or communities and usually live isolated with someone who is often the chronic victim of their rage; or they move around a lot, wearing out their welcome after relatively short periods of time in one place. While we may view others' rage as being out of control, those who are ragers feel very much in control and powerful. They no longer feel inadequate and defective.

Rage is intended to protect against further experiences of pain. Rage is a way of actively compensating for powerlessness and feelings of shame by offering a false, but attractive (to the rager) sense of power. When rage is the only way people know to protect against their emptiness, their powerlessness, and their pain, their choice is a quick one. Rage also offers protection, in that rageful behavior keeps people at a distance. As a result, other people cannot see into the raging person's inner self that he or she believes to be so ugly.

Rage as a defense offers protection not only by keeping others away, but also by transferring the shame to them. The outwardly rageful person chooses a victim-like person who, consciously or not, is willing to take the abuse and take on or assume the shame.   Rage can be accumulated anger that has never seemed safe to expose.

When anger is not safe, it becomes internalized, and with time it grows, festering into chronic bitterness, or even more likely, chronic depression, as we will discuss next.   When there has been no outlet for rage, it is more apt to explode suddenly as a significant single hostile act such as physical abuse, even a murder. Such an act is the consequence of the accumulation of feelings without the skills to tolerate painful feelings, to resolve conflict, or to perceive options and choices.

Depression As A Response To Pain

Unfortunately, a depressed person is typically pictured as one who sleeps excessively, maybe eighteen hours per day, is unable to eat, and is suicidal. While that picture represents the severe end of the depression continuum, most adults from troubled families who are depressed are able to function daily, meeting their required responsibilities. After all, that has been their survival mode.

When feelings cannot be expressed and so a person's emotions must necessarily be shut down, this naturally leads to depression. The false self that adult survivors present to the world may not have the look of depression, but their true self, their mental and emotional self, is experiencing great despair. "Looking good" children, as described in *It Will Never Happen To Me*, maintain the outward appearance of "doing just fine while dying on the inside." These are people who, like an addicted person, manipulate life so their true self cannot be seen. They are what I call "closeted depressed."

To keep depression hidden, those of us who are depressed avoid getting close enough or spending enough time around others who may recognize our true feelings and the pervasive emptiness our depression is masking. Nor do we develop close friendships where others are invested enough to "pull our covers." We appear very capable and seem to put out an impenetrable force field that says, "Don't ask me about me. Don't push me." It is difficult enough being depressed. It is even more difficult when we have shame around it — shame as one cause of depression, added shame because we are depressed.

There are many different theories about the cause of depression. Some clinicians and researchers believe it to be a biochemical imbalance, a disordered neurochemistry, best treated with antidepressants. It is commonly accepted among professionals that depression tends to run in families, suggesting there may be a physiological predisposition towards depression. Yet, many other theories support the belief that depression is a consequence of a habitually pessimistic and disordered way of viewing the world and is a consequence of loss and the inability to do the griefwork necessary to bring completion to the feelings of sorrow.   [Note: All depression needs to be assessed by a qualified physician.]

There is tremendous loss associated with being raised in a shame-based family. With the family being denial-centered, as it often is, and it not being okay to talk honestly, the sense of loss is amplified because there is no way to work through the pain. The hurt, the disappointment, the fears, and the angers associated with life events as well as with abandonment experiences are all swirled together and internalized. When you add to this a personal belief that says you are at fault, it is easy to see why you came to believe that you are not worthy, and so try to hide your real self from others. Also, you can see that eventually, whether you are thirty-five or fifty-five, suddenly you hit a wall. The burden of hiding eventually becomes too heavy, and all of those protecting, con-trolling mechanisms that kept you going for so long just stop working. The depression is there.

Most people who experience depression related to loss are extremely frightened of their feelings. And they have so much to feel about. When it is not safe to speak these feelings, they become directed inward against the self. This becomes another means of perpetuating shame, which then further protracts the depressive mood.

As discussed in chapter 1, there are necessary and unneces-sary losses in life. Because it was not safe to acknowledge them, we didn't learn coping skills for the loss that would occur in our adult years. So, when loss occurs and/or accumulates in adult-hood, we resort to the same defenses we have always used to deny what we are feeling.

When we have incredible grief and loss in our lives, many of us develop thought processes wherein we catastrophize and exag-gerate fear to such a point that we feel hopeless and in despair. For example, when your husband is twenty minutes late for an important appointment, you think he must have been in a terrible car accident. When your boss forgot to say hello, you feel certain that she is angry with you and is going to let you go. Given some small bit of knowledge, we presume the worst will happen.

Over the years, given our experiences, we have developed a committee of internal voices that have become our Inner Critic, telling ourselves we are stupid, not wanted, ugly, and not important, in response to any slight or perceived loss, or when not being fully embraced by someone we value.

Most adults from troubled families experience a combination of both—unresolved loss and a pessimistic view of life. When we feel our powerlessness, our despair, and our fear, we send ourselves into a downhill spiral so quickly anybody's head would be spinning.

Acute Episodes Of Depression

Many adults make their way through life cut off from their internal pain, until they experience an important present-day loss—the last child leaving home, a significant health problem, the death of a close friend or family member, the loss of job or career opportunity. As great numbers of women enter perimenopausal and menopausal stages, the combination of physical changes and the symbolism around such changes can create an incredible sense of loss. For men and women both, one significant present loss can be the straw that breaks the camel's back. In other words, that current loss can trigger the beginning of a downward emotional spiral in which the adult becomes overwhelmed in despair, shame, powerlessness, and depression.

Sally, who was raised in a physically abusive home, was a department manager in an engineering firm. She had tucked away the pain of her childhood history into a corner of her heart and put a lock on it. She was involved in raising her own family, and kept a distant relationship with her sister and parents. All aspects of her life were compartmentalized. Then one day, she lost her oldest daughter in an accident, and six months after that, her father died. Three weeks later, Sally made her first suicide attempt. To lose a child is one of life's greatest tragedies for anybody. Further, Sally had no skills, no internal supports to deal with the intense pain when her daughter died. While she did not feel close to her father, his death unleashed all of the childhood pain she had so neatly and quietly tucked away. When present-day loss occurs, we may not be aware of remembering our growing up years, but we are certainly feeling the accumulated pain.

Tom, who was raised in an extremely critical home and felt his loss through chronic rejection, quickly separated from his parents and all his siblings after high school. Then, at the age of twenty-eight when his fiancee broke up with him, his exaggerated and catastrophic thinking led into incredible despair. He had talked himself into seeing himself as totally unworthy. He envisioned that his fiancee would marry someone much more financially stable than he was and certainly a lot more fun and exciting. She would have children with someone else. He would be alone all of his life. He was convinced he would never find happiness. He would never be able to offer anything to anyone else anyway. On and on and on Tom's incredibly painful thinking continued. Soon, he was sleeping twelve to fourteen hours a day, missing days at work, and no longer exercising or eating properly.

Losing a relationship, particularly in young adulthood, happens to many of us. However, because of chronic losses in his childhood, Tom had not learned the skills needed to grieve through the loss of his fiancee. He was not able to understand the experience in any way except as further evidence of his inadequacy and worth-lessness. This loss was simply one more that added fuel to his already existing fire of shame.

Like victimization, depression is a consequence of the inability to defend and protect ourselves against the pain of loss.

Suicide: The Most Severe Response To Pain

"I am hopeless. I am unworthy and I don't deserve to live. Life won't get any better and I can't stand this pain." Suicidal thoughts, attempts, and completions speak of many issues. They are often a reflection of anger and rage turned inward and of depression.

For some people, the act of suicide seems to claim power to compensate for their powerlessness in life. For others, death is perceived to be a better option than to live with certain memories and shame. The pain is too overwhelming, and out of despair and hopelessness, people become their own victims. Thoughts of taking our own lives are much more prevalent than people realize. While pain creates such thoughts, we also experience shame for having the thoughts. My message to you is, Please don't feel ashamed. But, please do speak up and let someone know how frightened, angry, or hopeless you are feeling.

In recovery, you CAN speak about those issues that have created the pain. You CAN say NO to your shame. You CAN learn to find ways to express your anger without hurting yourself. You CAN develop new beliefs and behaviors that support you in the way you deserve to be supported. You CAN learn how to access the power within you that does exist. You deserve to be able to live without pain. But when you are considering suicide as a way out of your pain, you must reach out and get assistance from a helping professional.

BEHAVIORAL RESPONSES TO PAIN

"Medicating" Pain

Along with the ways we feel our past and past-driven present pain, whether our emotional response is one of victimization, rage, or depression, we may also try different behaviors to control our pain, hoping to lessen the hurt. Unfortunately, our efforts to control the pain don't remove the cause or source of our feeling. One way people try to control and regulate their pain is by "medicating" it through addiction to substances or compulsive behaviors.

Addictions

Types of addictions may range from chemical dependency to food, to caffeine, nicotine, sugar, alcohol, and other drugs. Many of the substances people become addicted to are socially sanctioned and supported, making it very difficult for those abusing them to see how they are using them in unhealthy ways. [Note: In terms of ending specific addictions, in nearly all cases abstinence is the goal.   Also, it is vital to recognize that once someone is addicted, will power or self control is no longer a relevant issue.]

In addition to temporarily controlling our pain, the substances we use and abuse very often provide something for us we do not know how to seek naturally. As an example, alcohol may give a sense of power to someone who has only known powerlessness.

27

It may give access to a sense of courage and confidence to someone who feels lacking. This is certainly drug-induced and false, but for many people, false is better than none. For someone who is isolated and feels alienated from others, alcohol makes it easier to reach out to people. "Give me a little bit to drink and I become alive. I pull myself away from the wall and I find myself talking, laughing, listening. I see people responding to me and I like it." This kind of thinking doesn't mean that a person is addicted, but it does mean he or she is thirsty for connection with others. This person has expressed a need for psychological reinforcement in order to feel whole and complete.

For people who have never taken time for play or laughter because life has been so serious and "I have to get things done," alcohol gives them the opportunity to relax. Alice identified, "My entire life has been spent taking care of other people. I am always busy. I make these lists daily, thinking the world will stop if I don't get the job done. I don't think about missing out on fun — it has never been a part of my life.

"I was a teetotaler. I never drank until I was twenty-six. I don't even know why I started. But those first few times I remember thinking that I was being silly, hearing myself laugh with other people. It actually scared me. Yet, at the same time there was this attraction. It was as if there was this whole other part of me I didn't know and maybe was okay to know."

"The attraction to relaxing with alcohol kept getting stronger. I can actually remember thinking, 'I don't have to make this decision tonight,' or 'I don't have to do this by myself.' Pretty soon it was, 'I don't have to do this at all.' I was having fun. I was relaxing." While Alice's new ways of letting go and becoming less rigid were not harmful, because she did not know how to do it without alcohol, she ultimately became dependent on it. Alice, like so many others, was seeking wholeness. But the only glimpse she had of it was "under the influence."

Variations of this scenario fit for other addictions. Our relation-ship to certain foods or the intake, lack of intake, and/or purging of food may be about an internal struggle with power and control. We may be attempting to access power that we don't have the skills or confidence to access more naturally. Starving ourselves, purging, and compulsive overeating may be anger turned toward ourselves. Possibly we are punishing ourselves for being bad. The anorexic may be literally starving herself to become invisible in response to shame; the anorexic and bulimic may be seeking perfection — which is based in shame.

When we come from a pain-based family, it is common to go outside of ourselves for a quick answer to relieve our suffering. It doesn't seem possible that we have any way to help ourselves. Yet, ultimately, we can keep our pain under control only so long before it starts to leak out. Frightened, we feel out of control and we seek a medicator. Sometimes that medicator is a person; it could possibly be an activity; many times it is a substance. Often it is a combination of compulsions and addictions.

Compulsions

To experience shame and powerlessness is to be in intolerable pain. While physical pain is horrible, there are moments of relief. There is hope of being cured. However, with shame when we believe we are defective, there is no cure; shame is a defeated state. We have no relationship with ourselves or anyone else; we are totally alone. Relief from this intolerable pain must come, one way or another. We need someone or something to take away our profound loneliness and fear, and so we assume we need a mood-altering experience. We need an escape. Everyone has certain behaviors used as a way to "escape," but it is when we come to depend on them to relieve our unworthiness that these become compulsive in nature. And when we grow up in an environment of shaming, where the cause of pain is external, we develop the belief that the solutions to problems exist only externally, i.e., substances or behaviors that are medicators.

There are many different types of addictions and compulsions ranging from compulsively repeated activities, to preoccupying thoughts, to relationship dependencies. We use some form of keeping busy to distance or to distract ourselves, to get our minds off our pain, our fear, or our anger. We keep busy to stay in control of our feelings and therefore to avoid feeling bad. Many behavioral compulsions would be otherwise harmless activities if they weren't exaggerated, destroying the balance in our lives. For example, exercise is a healthy activity until done so excessively that we actually injure our bodies.

Relationship addiction is the dependence on being in a relationship to provide our worth. That means we use other people to lessen our shame and to avoid truly facing our selves.

Sex addiction is the use of sexual stimulation to act as a detractor or medicator of pain; or it may be a false way of accessing power to overcome our sense of powerlessness. Compulsive sex experiences can temporarily offer us warmth and an appearance of love. Or we can act out sex as an expression of anger. These sex experiences may temporarily affirm that we are lovable and worthy, all the while compounding our belief in our defectiveness. Sex addicts vary in their focus, from obsessive masturbating, using pornographic materials, exhibitionism, obscene phone calls, voyeurism, multiple affairs, and so on. For sex addicts, certain behaviors take on sexual meaning; they view objects and people through their preoccupation.

Even though compulsive behaviors distract and alter feelings, feelings themselves can become compulsive in nature. We become dependent on certain feelings to mask and avoid experiencing what we are really feeling. We may become a rageaholic, using rage as a release for all feelings. Fear can overwhelm us, where phobias, hypervigilance, and/or anxieties can control our lives.

While some compulsions are certainly more harmful to ourselves and our family, others may be considered only nuisances. Substances and behaviors can detract from, medicate and/or anesthetize our pain. Yet, any time we use a substance or become involved in a process or behavior that interferes with our honesty, our ability to be present with ourselves, it deserves our attention.

RATIONAL OR COGNITIVE RESPONSES TO PAIN

While some people focus on controlling the pain itself, others attempt to control the source of the pain. Control is the key word here. These people hope to control the cause of the pain, as opposed to removing, releasing, or healing it. As with the emotional and behavioral responses discussed earlier, these cognitive or rational responses try to prevent potential abandonment and prevent the possibility of exposing their shameful selves.

Perfectionism

Our common rational or cognitive response to pain is perfectionism. Perfectionism is driven by the belief that if a person's behavior is perfect, there will be no reason to be criticized and therefore no more cause for pain. However, perfectionism is a shame-based phenomenon because children learn that "no matter what they do, it's never good enough." As a result, in their struggle to feel good about themselves and relieve the source of pain, they constantly push to excel, to be the best.

Highly perfectionistic people are usually people who have been raised in a rigid family environment. The rigidity may be in the form of unrealistic expectations that parents have for their children and/or for themselves. Either way, the parents' expectations are internalized by the children. Also, rigidity may be expressed as children feel the need to do things "right" in order to get approval from their parent and to lessen fears of rejection. For most children, being "right" is perceived to mean there was no room for mistakes.

Let's look at the example of Teri, nineteen years old, in a therapy group and talking about being a perfectionist. When she was in junior high school, she related, in order to be able to visit with friends on Saturday afternoon, she had to complete certain household tasks. So, every Saturday morning she would approach her father to get a list of what she needed to accomplish to be able to go out later in the day. She'd get her typewritten list and go on about her duties. When the list was completed, she'd return it to her father, but at this point, he'd give her a second list. When she was done with that list, he inevitably gave her a third list. Often times a fourth and fifth list.

As you can guess, Teri didn't spend a lot of Saturday afternoons with her friends. When Teri told this story, tears streamed down her cheeks. Then she paused and reflectively commented, "But we all come from some pretty crazy families. It could have been worse. Besides I learned a few things. If you want something done, ask me. I know how to be quick." Then haltingly she added, "What I really learned was that no matter what I do, it's never good enough."

That was the lesson for Teri. No matter what she did, it wasn't good enough. But what Teri did need to learn is that whether or not she was permitted to spend time with her friends was not about how well or how quick she was in her work. Nothing was good enough, because it wasn't humanly possible to please her father. This Saturday ritual was not about Teri. It was about her father and his need to control, his need for power. Ultimately, for her own well-being, Teri needed to acknowledge that. In doing so, she would be able to establish an emotional boundary, separating her worth from her father's criticism.

Unfortunately, most perfectionists have no internal sense of limits. With shame and fear nipping at their heels the entire time, they always perceive their performance as related to a standard or judgment outside themselves. As children, they were taught to strive onward. There was never a time or place to rest or to have inner joy and satisfaction.

Perfection as a performance criteria means you never measure up. Then, not measuring up is translated into a comparison with others of good versus bad, better versus worse. Inevitably you end up feeling the lesser for the comparison. Comparison with others is one of the primary ways that people continue to create more shame for themselves. You continue to do to yourself on the inside what was done to you from the outside. Since your efforts were never experienced as sufficient, adequate, or good enough, you did not develop an internal sense of how much is good enough.

As adults, we need to identify those areas where we once strived so hard for recognition, attention, and approval. Then we need to recognize that not only did we do our best, we truly were good enough. The lack of acceptance we have felt is not about us or our worth, but about those who judged us and who also sought to feel a sense of power by threatening to reject us. While we were not able to understand that as children, we can come to terms with that today.

Procrastination And Ambivalence

Procrastination, such as starting but not completing a project, or considering a project but never initiating it, is often an attempt to defend against further shame. Perfectionism and procrastination are closely linked. It is easy to picture Teri, in the above example, never finishing her first list, realizing that she could not please her father. Teri, though, believed in herself a bit more strongly than most people who procrastinate. Often, the procrastinator has little confidence and more fear. The perfectionist is more apt to follow through because there is the possibility of the reinforcement of some sense of accomplishment. The procrastinator will not even see that possibility.

Some children received so little attention that they were not encouraged to initiate projects, let alone to complete them. Too many times when these children did something, drew a picture or wrote a story, and gleefully showed their parents, the parents barely looked at it and then set it aside, or maybe even lost it. When there is no positive reinforcement to complete school projects or homework, children perform with ambivalence. They believe that "No one else cares," and develop the attitude, "Why should I care?" The result is procrastination and ambivalence.

It was just as painful for children when their parents did pay attention, but were constantly critical, maybe making a joke of the children's work, possibly humiliating them in front of others. Sue, who was an average student in school, became very excited about a history project during her sophomore year of high school. "I worked hard on it all quarter, which was unusual for me, but I found this real interesting and the teacher liked me, so I really wanted to do well. One night I was at the dining room table putting all of the pages of my report in a notebook to be turned in the next day in class. I wasn't expecting my parents to come home for a few hours yet, so I was shocked when my mother and stepfather came in, both laughing loudly, both drunk. Mom asked what I was doing and then picked up my paper which was titled "Did America Need To Be In World War II?" Suddenly, she was in a rage and calling me a communist, saying I wasn't patriotic.

"It was unreal. Within minutes, they were both screaming at me calling me all kinds of names. They took my report and, in their words, threw the 'trash' into the fireplace. Well, there was no way I could tell the teacher what had happened. I just took a failing grade. It was pretty horrifying, but I should have known not to put that much effort into anything. Most things never worked out for me too much."

Sue's sense of defeat was a culmination of similar experiences. Whenever she put forth effort to achieve, she somehow always felt diminished. It was several years before she could put into perspective the report incident and all the smaller incidents that led her to believe even if she wanted to work at something, it probably wasn't worth the effort. As a result, Sue quit trying to achieve at a very young age.

When children are humiliated for their efforts, made to feel inadequate or stupid, they find ways to protect themselves so they can't do something that would prove they really are a failure.

In addition, children become discouraged when they are constantly compared to someone who "did it better" or might have done it better. Tom says he was always compared to his two older brothers. "My two older brothers were articulate. They were quick and did well in school. It took me longer to grasp things. I wasn't as interested in math and sciences as they were. I was more interested in my friends. So, with school being more of a struggle and having no real help from my parents, only the push that 'you should be like your brothers,' I just gave up. I wasn't like them and didn't feel I could be."

Also mixed into procrastination can be anger, expressed as an attitude of "I'll show you — I won't finish this," or "I'll only do it part way. I won't give my best." Inherent in this attitude is a challenge that insists, "Like me for who I am, not for what I do." In a family where rigidity is the rule, where it is not okay to make mistakes, not okay to take risks or be different, not okay to draw attention to yourself, you learn not to initiate, or not to finish what you started. For those of us raised this way, it is amazing that we get anything done.

Understanding Your Defenses Against Pain

Rage, depression, victimization, addictions, compulsions, perfectionism, and procrastination — these are some of the responses, which are results of having lived with fear and pain. They often became protectors. They offered to control the pain itself and/or control the source of the pain. Other protectors begin as common, everyday acts, but taken to extremes create negative outcomes in the long run. Some of these are intellectualization, physical isolation, humor, magical thinking, lying, silence, and withdrawal.

What are the defenses you employ? It would be helpful for you to make a list of defenses you developed to defend against the pain. Are those still behaviors you use today? After you make your list, then ask yourself the following questions:

- What did it [the protective behavior] do for you in the past?
- What is it doing for you now?
- Would you like to let go of it?
- What do you need to do to let it go?
- What is interfering with your ability to let go of it?

LETTING GO OF THE PAST, HEALING THE PAIN

Every one of us would like to rid ourselves of pain. The answer lies in being willing to admit and show your pain. That means facing the feelings. It means being willing to own the sadness, the hurt and the fears, embarrassments and anger about how you have had to live your life. It means being willing to be specific about all the ways you fought for emotional survivorship, how you attempted to compensate for powerlessness, how you tried to gain control, to overcome the incredible sense of shame and fear that have been so significant in your life, in the past and the past-driven present.

LOSS EXPERIENCES AS ADULTS

Creating A Loss Graph For Your Adult Years

Ultimately, you will need to identify the loss events, conditions, and shaming messages in your adult life, as well as those in your growing up years, in order to be able to become separate from them. An adult loss graph, like the loss graph of your early years, is a very useful way to begin to identify the difference between who you are and what has happened to you.

To create a loss graph for your adult years, you will need to record the loss events you experienced as an adult, your age at the time, and the feelings that you remember having when the losses occurred. Also, you need to record loss conditions and abandonment experiences and feelings that have been a part of your adult life. When you create this loss graph, remember that you are trying to record your adult experiences — not those you remember having happened when you were a child. Loss conditions, however, are different from loss events and abandonment experiences. A condition is a state that exists over time, so adult loss conditions may very likely include unresolved childhood conditions. If your childhood losses are still creating pain for you

in the present, then this is a very real condition in your adult life.

Loss Graph For Adult Years
Joyce

Loss Events	Miscarriage	Divorce	Left college prematurely due to stress	Aware of marital infidelity	Loses job promotion
Age	21	23	24	36	38
Unattended Feelings	Despair	Despair fear	Sad frightened insecure	Anger	Despair

Loss conditions in Family:	Unresolved childhood pain; Emotionally abusive partner; Compulsive overeater.	Abandonment Experiences/Feelings:		Inadequate; frightened; sad; ashamed; anger.

Joyce carried into adulthood the unresolved feelings of her childhood. Added to this, was the pain of adult loss events, pain which she had not yet learned to work through. The feelings were there, but she was unable to attend to them. In addition, she chose a partner that fueled her sense of shame and abandonment. Her compulsive overeating only heightened the accumulation of these feelings. Except for her compulsive overeating, most people saw Joyce as a happily married mother of two daughters, who worked as a medical records specialist in a community hospital.

Joyce's loss graph, however, offers a strong, visual record of pain, a striking contrast to her public image.

Loss Graph For Adult Years
Tim

Loss Events	Engagement broken	Loses job	Son, 6 years old, diagnosed w/ cancer
Age	24	26	36
Unattended Feelings	Angry sad	Angry frightened	Frightened sad

Loss Conditions in Family:	Unresolved childhood and Viet Nam pain; Wife depressed; Chronic conflict around child's loss of health.	Abandonment Experiences/Feelings:	sadness; fear; futility.

Like Joyce, Tim never worked through the pain of major loss events in his youth, such as his brother's death and his own Viet Nam service. Consequently, as an adult, Tim carried pain from the past, compounded by severe loss conditions in his own family, especially his son's serious illness. At the age of thirty-six, Tim struggled to present himself to the world as a man who loved his family and enjoyed his work as a media technician at a local television station. But, because Tim never learned the emotional skills to heal his feelings, his loss graph clearly depicts a heavy burden of past and present pain.

Joyce and Tim may each continue to carry their increasingly heavy burdens of pain until, one day, they simply can't go on any longer. Or, instead, they may become aware that there is another way of being and another way of dealing with their feelings. With that awareness, that world-view shift, they will be able to turn to a new course for their lives.

Setting Boundaries To Regain Your Power

Once your loss graphs are complete, you have a very graphic representation of your pain and, because you haven't learned the skills to heal your pain, you are also looking at a depiction of your powerlessness. Faced with this picture of your plight, but at the same time, aware now that you can choose a different way of being, where do you begin? One of the first steps is to develop boundaries. Boundaries will give you back your power.

Boundaries are the mechanisms that bring safety into our lives by establishing healthy control. Boundaries are statements about what we will and will not do. Boundaries act as limits for what others can and cannot do to us. By setting boundaries for our-selves, we are exercising our inherent power to declare that we are autonomous individuals in our own right, not possessions or extensions of anyone else.

As a child, you had little power to determine your interactions with the world. You had no way to defend against boundary invasions. Yet, being invaded — used, abused, or violated — you believed you had no personal worth, having been treated as an object or possession, not a person. You may also have believed you were bad or weak because you couldn't stand up for yourself. Believing you are worthless and bad causes tremendous pain. But, now that you are an adult, you can develop and strengthen boundaries, which will give you inner power, and will help heal the old pain.

To let go of the pain, we will have to walk through it to finish it, but we do not have to walk through the pain alone again, as helpless, vulnerable children. But, remember, whatever you experienced as a child, your perceptions and interpretations were those of a child. The perceived belief that you were worthless or bad was not true. You never were bad or unworthy, and you are not today. It is my hope that, in time, you will be able to say and to believe in your heart, "I am good. I am adequate. I am worthy."

WE CAN'T GO FORWARD WITHOUT FINISHING THE PAST

To go forward, we must finish and let go of the past. Jill Johnston, author of *Mother Bound*, writes that as we let go of the past, "we alter the way we see ourselves in the present and the way we cast ourselves into the future...The notion of who has rights, whose voice can be heard, whose individuality is worthy, comes under revision...and the shame of difference will evaporate."

To let go of our pain, we must also acknowledge what we have been doing in the present to control our pain. Facing our own painful reality, both past and present, empowers us by giving us choice.

One option is that we can remain role-players, acting out old family roles, directed by negative judgments and false beliefs about ourselves. Choosing this option, of course, we are not really attempting to finish the past. Also, we are consigning ourselves to a future weighted down by the need to manage our shame and pain.

The other option we have is to become free agents, choosing to set our own course, act according to our own freely chosen beliefs, rather than the dictates of external standards. On this course, we are able to finish the past because we are no longer being controlled by it.

Finishing the past does not mean that it disappears from our memories. Instead, it simply takes its rightful place as one significant dimension of our personal history. And as we release ourselves from the punishing restrictions from our past, our pain is relieved as well. Very simply, if the cause of pain is removed, the pain will subside and then come to an end.

Letting go of our pain doesn't mean that we will, or should be able to forget our suffering. That would be another kind of denial. But, in time we can learn to honor our past pain much as we would honor a soldier returning from war. We can also honor our experience as a significant part of our life's struggle to grow and survive.

Freeing ourselves from pain is what recovery is all about. Releasing ourselves from the past and freeing ourselves from the painful limitations of a past-driven, present life is the process we go through as we turn to the new reality we want. Remember that recovery takes time. But it can be done. It can happen to you, to me, to all of us.

The awarenesses we now have bring us to another turning point to recovery:

The pain we feel is not only from the past, but also from the past-driven present.

We were powerless in the past, but we are not powerless in the present.

Another turning point comes with another awareness:

We are not our pain.

We are much, much more than mere embodiments of pain. Realizing that truth allows us to separate our selves from our emotional responses. Further, our own response is something we can affect, something we can make a choice about. As Steven Covey writes, "Responsibility is response-ability."

Together, these awarenesses lead us to the turning point that can put us on the path of freedom:

Our pain is our responsibility.

What we do about our pain is a choice we make.

Adult Children of Alcoholics: An Expanded Framework for Assessment and Diagnosis

Stephanie Brown, Ph.D.

I. INTRODUCTION: THE BIRTH OF A CONCEPT

The field of alcoholism, or chemical dependence, has undergone tremendous change over the last 15 years. Today, it is hard to conceive of a time when the concepts "adult children of alcohol- ics" or "codependence" didn't exist. These terms have been established quickly in popular and clinical language, labeling a particular kind of patient and treatment for at least ten years.

The popular movement (including the mass media, lay confer- ences, and trade books) named and described a phenomenon never before legitimized. Academic theoreticians and clinicians of all disciplines simply had never considered the impact of one individual's alcoholism on another, which is precisely what the popular movement accomplished. This shift in perspective—from a singular focus on the alcoholic as identified patient to a broader interactive systems focus on the family and other individuals within the family—has dramatically affected popular and profes- sional thinking about health and illness. At this point, nothing is clear, and our understanding of chemical dependence, though no longer hidden and denied, is muddy, vague, and full of serious problems. Just what is a codependent? An ACA? What do these terms mean and how can we best use them to clarify our thinking and our treatments? In this paper, we will examine the origin and evolutionary development of these terms, outlining problems with both and radical suggestions for improvement.

Next, we will leave "codependence" behind and focus on ACAs, arguing that the term ACA be used descriptively and not as a singular diagnostic entity. We will look at the commonalities of ACA themes in treatment, which mistakenly have been generalized to an ACA diagnosis. I will propose that the ACA label, and our new understanding of the impact of trauma and systems dynamics on individual development, demand an expansion in our thinking to include multi-level developmental diagnostic tracks.

We can identify three separate assessment tracks illuminated by the concept ACA: 1) the childhood alcoholic family environment, including the reality of trauma; 2) the family system, organized to both deny and maintain the reality of parental alcoholism; and 3) the nature of attachment within this environment and system and its impact on individual development. Taken together, this expanded framework constitutes a much fuller, deeper understanding of child and adult development and adaptation.

Surprisingly, multi-track theory is a revolutionary idea, both in popular thinking and in academic circles. We simply have no means to integrate multiple theories because we have been so committed to an individual diagnostic framework. The drive to define codependence and ACA as individual diagnostic entities reinforces this narrow, reductionistic bias. It is time to challenge this favored view and expand our thinking, even though it means giving up simple cookbook formulas for change.

Popular, revolutionary concepts that literally blew the lid off of denial at a national level are already limited and restrictive. It is up to academia and clinicians to make sense of these ideas by tackling their inherent complexity rather than succumbing to an equally global, vague and ultimately meaningless singular diagnosis.

II. WHAT IS CODEPENDENCE?

Origins of the Term

The origin of the idea "codependence" goes back to the 1950s when Al-Anon, the autonomous arm of Alcoholics Anonymous (AA) designed for the spouse of an alcoholic was born (Al-Anon, 1984). Al-Anon provided the first official recognition that alcoholism has an impact on others. Until this time, all attention had been on the drinking alcoholic, as if that individual and the alcoholism existed in a vacuum.

Like AA, the focus of Al-Anon was on the individual, but it was clearly the individual in an interpersonal, familial context. In a similar program to the twelve steps of AA, Al-Anon provides instruction in how to detach and disengage from maladaptive and unhealthy reactions to the alcoholic in the same way that the drinker relinquishes alcohol.

At the same time Al-Anon was developing, Joan Jackson (1954; 1962) outlined stages in a developmental process of alcoholism for the spouse, similar to the stages of the disease process defined for the alcoholic by E.M. Jellinek (1960). Prior to Jackson's work, research on the family focused only on personality traits or the role of the wife, who was thought to cause, perpetuate, or reinforce the alcoholism of her mate (at this time thought to be almost entirely men). Jackson reversed cause and effect, as did Vaillant much later (1982). Instead of starting out with problems that caused her husband's drinking, the wife's difficulties were now recognized to be a consequence of or a response to his drinking.

A Family Disease

The disease concept, just gaining acceptance in the 50s and 60s for the alcoholic, now translated into "family disease." The term "co-alcoholic" was coined to describe the partner and the focus broadened to include the interactions, adjustment and development of the family with an alcoholic member. Co-alcoholics learned that they were part of a disease process bigger than any one individual. While they were now relieved of the responsibility for causing the alcoholism of their mates, they were learning instead that their reactive response (which was co-alcoholism) was unhealthy for them and ineffective in changing the drinker.

The Alcoholic Family: Systems Theory

Peter Steinglass (1980; 1987) shifted the emphasis from a disease model to exploration of interactional systems dynamics in developing the concept of the alcoholic family. He and Brown (1977; 1985; 1988; 1991) described the alcoholism of a parent as a "central organizing principle" determining interactional patterns within the family. They suggested that parental alcoholism be viewed as a governing agent affecting the development of the family as a whole and individuals within. Until now, co-alcoholism applied only to the alcoholic's mate. The systems concept of an alcoholic family paved the way for including children.

The Value of Co-Alcoholism

As a systems term, specific to alcoholism and the response to it, co-alcoholism was extremely useful. Appropriately negative, the term described the mutual reinforcement of pathological systems dynamics. When limited to interactional alcoholic dynamics, the implicit dichotomous all-or-none frame was also appropriate. In any dyad governed by one partner's alcoholism, there was an alcoholic — who was dominant — and a co-alcoholic, who was submissive and reactive to the dominance of the drinker. Family systems dynamics, including the maintenance of family homeo-stasis, evolved around the pathology of active alcoholism and the couple's or family's efforts to sustain it. In family systems theory, this dominant-submissive system was analogous to polarized, highly skewed, schismatic families, or enmeshed or hostile depen-dent systems (Framo, 1965; Minuchin, 1974; Bader & Pearson, 1988).

From an individual perspective, the co-alcoholic was someone who subordinated or literally forfeited an independent self—feelings, perceptions, beliefs, and explanations of reality—in favor of the alcoholic and the larger pathological alcoholic system (Brown 1988).

Codependence

With the birth of the COA movement and the application of family systems theory to alcoholism, the term co-alcoholism was broadened to codependence, referring now to any reactive, submissive response to the dominance of another (Brown, 1988). Implicit in this generalized view was the loss of self to another's control. Why would anyone go along with such a sacrifice? We will see later that the human need for attachment is so powerful and so basic as to make this kind of accommodation to another quite common and part of normal behavior.

That is why this terminology is so problematic. Like co-alcohol-ism, codependence is an exclusively negative term which turns much of normal human behavior into pathology.

The reactive codependent stance defines the individual as a passive victim, while its opposite—the dependent—is ironically seen to be the aggressor. In fact, both terms deal with dependence and need in humans. The dependent person is seen to be overtly needy and demanding, while the codependent is seen to sacrifice all claim to personal need. From an interactional perspective, the codependent satisfies dependency needs just like the dependent individual. It is simply more disguised.

This framework misses entirely the long-accepted developmental and psychodynamic view (Rolf et al, 1990) that all human beings are engaged in dynamic interaction with others and their environment. Individuals are not passive recipients as the dichotomous dependent-codependent frame suggests.

The fact that all individuals are actively engaged does not mean they are to blame, a faulty conclusion unfortunately drawn by many when the passive "victim" status of codependence is challenged. In fact, to counter this faulty trap of blaming the victim, popular thinking simply reverses it, now holding abusive parents or partners responsible for all disappointments in childhood or adult relationships. Neither "solution" helps anybody out of the dichotomous trap.

In the current frame, the dependent-codependent system is pathological, making both partners victims to a system they actively participate in maintaining. Why and how they do this is related to attachment and issues of normal human development which we will look at later.

Negative Bias

The terms dependence and codependence are exclusively negative, reflecting our cultural preference for "self-sufficiency" and our distaste for need in any form. Thus, we have totally eliminated the option for healthy, positive dependency or caretaking reactivity. With this restrictive, negative terminology, we have further eliminated the possibility of healthy interdependence, a fluid and flexible interactional system in which both partners are capable of "give and take" and both roles are valued.

The unhealthy dependent-codependent framework makes our human values of kindness, altruism and self-sacrifice totally suspect. By offering no positive options and equating dependence with failure and unhealthy need, we have successfully pathologized the entire human race.

Elsewhere (Brown 1991), I have proposed a solution to this dilemma, if we must keep the basic terminology. In essence, we could add a modifier, distinguishing between healthy and unhealthy dependence and healthy and unhealthy codependence. It is a simple solution, but difficult to implement because it requires a capacity to recognize and tolerate "shades of gray" or ambiguity, a cognitive and emotional flexibility that is missing or restricted in many people. Thus, the all or none polarity of the dependent-codependent frame appeals to the need for rigid, air-tight right and wrong classifications. Unfortunately, both options in this dichotomy are "wrong" and there is no way to get it "right."

Other Problems: Over-Generalization and Over-Simplification

Ideally, clinical terminology should clarify distinctions or diagnostic entities. The term codependence does the opposite, virtually obliterating differences. It crosses theoretical frames, defining systems dynamics as individual pathology. It also moves from psychology to sociology. Epstein and Epstein (1990) argue that codependence is "social narrative," a comment on the values and mores of the culture. They suggest that traditional masculine and feminine roles of dominance and submission are being challenged by pathologizing them to aggressor and victim.

The term crosses turf in other ways. Codependence can now be applied as a noun, an adjective or a verb. People can be codependents, they can behave in a "codependent manner," or they can "co" another individual, all of which are negative.

Perhaps the worst over-generalization is the crossover that equates codependents and ACAs on the basis of the shared reactive position in relation to a dominant other. An early paper by Greenleaf (1981) suggests the folly of this condensation in understanding the interpersonal dynamics within the alcoholic family.

Greenleaf suggests distinguishing between the co-alcoholic and "para"-alcoholic to underscore the different origins and functions of a reactive stance in adults and children.

The terms codependent and ACA are simply not interchangeable. Codependence refers to adult status, a submissive "partner," while para-alcoholism, or ACA, refers back to childhood to the impact and consequences of growing up with parental alcoholism. It is essential to make distinctions between adult and child status.

What to do?

Although I have suggested the possibility of an expanded framework to include healthy and unhealthy codependence (Brown, 1991), I will advocate an extreme position for purposes of this paper, to underscore the enormous problems we have created and continue to reinforce. As lay and professional, we are caught in a thinking disorder similar to the pathology of the alcoholic family. We are over-generalizing and over-simplifying in order to make sense of cherished terms. By attempting to create a singular individual diagnosis of codependence or ACA, we are blurring, denying and rationalizing away vast significant differences between individuals and between experiences.

I recommend limiting the use of the term codependence to the interactional systems dynamics of alcoholism and chemical dependence. I recommend abandoning the use of the term to describe interactional patterns and systems dynamics not related to chemical addiction. By taking such a strong stance, we force ourselves to acknowledge the problems with our terminology and to start over. Such a position requires us to expand our thinking, to add a systems track and a separate, environmental, trauma track and to move away from a condensed individual diagnosis.

We are in danger of turning systems dynamics into individual pathology. If we continue with our faulty terminology and faulty logical premises, we will take the next "logical" but faulty step of equating the now global, vague, almost meaningless term of codependence with "relationship disorder."

In the next section, I will follow through on my own recommendation. Leaving codependence behind, I will outline a multi-level diagnostic framework for understanding ACAs. I will then illustrate how the multi-level and complex experiences of living with parental alcoholism affect the individual interpersonally. I will argue that the ACA experience requires massive defensive accommodation, the impact of which is felt most severely and acutely in interpersonal relationships.

III. WHAT IS AN ACA? COMMON THEMES

The term ACA started simultaneously in different parts of the country in the late seventies, predominantly in clinical settings. Brown and Cermak reported their initial findings of ACAs in interactional group therapy in 1979 (Brown and Cermak).

Others were also describing shared family experiences. Claudia Black focused on young children living with an alcoholic parent (Black, 1980). Newsweek magazine (1979) announced this new "idea" in its Lifestyle section, describing common experiences, as did charter statements of ACA lay associations (NACOA, 1983).

At this point, ACA had become an important description of a certain kind of family history characterized by common themes (Cermak and Brown, 1982) including chaos, uncertainty, and a changing reality. In interactional group therapy, ACAs demonstrated an overwhelming emphasis on issues of interpersonal safety, including long-standing serious problems with trust, guardedness, hyper-vigilance, a need for control and the fear of the loss of control, cognitive and affective denial, all-or-none thinking, and an overriding, inappropriate assumption of responsibility for others (Brown, 1986; 1988; 1991; Cermak and Brown, 1982), which Cermak (1986) later linked to post-traumatic stress disorder.

These clinical descriptions painted a portrait of alcoholic family life never previously acknowledged or legitimized. They established the "what-it-was-like" reality of parental alcoholism, literally describing what happens to children living in such an environment — that is, the kinds of experiences, sights and sounds that accompany parental alcoholism.

Black (1981) and Wegsheider (1981) added systems theory to the base of environmental description, outlining various role assignments children assume as a systemic accommodation to parental alcoholism.

The popular movement next made an inappropriate leap, going from common themes of childhood family history to individual adult diagnosis, based on a classification of shared personality traits (Woititz, 1983). Though well received at the public level, these characteristics reflected the over-simplification and over-generalization now characterizing the popular field. The shared personality traits, thought to differentiate ACAs from others, are actually part of all normal development and human behavior. Like the terms codependence and dependence, these traits are also exclusively negative when referring to the ACA experience.

The ACA movement got off track at this point, moving in the wrong direction toward individual diagnosis as the simplest way of fitting in with current accepted diagnostic standards. It did so understandably because DSM (1987), the official standard of practice, does not separate out or recognize environmental or systems pathology, either in etiology or consequence. But environmental and systems pathology were reflected in the themes. Nor does DSM have any mechanism to link childhood experiences with adult disturbance — a cause and effect connection implicit in the label "adult child."

In reducing ACA to an individual diagnosis, the popular movement missed its most important unforeseen impact: to lay bare the absence of any multi-level, integrated theory of child and adult development.

The early descriptions and identified treatment themes, plus the multi-level label "adult child" provide the guidelines for an expanded theory. In the remainder of this paper, I will outline three distinct assessment tracks suggested by these early themes: the environmental context, the system, and individual developmental perspectives. At this stage of theory development, these domains may be viewed loosely as "assessment tracks", each exerting separate and interactional influences on the child. We will then examine the experiences and the consequences of living with parental alcoholism for the child and adult within each domain. Finally, we will look at interpersonal problems for ACAs in close couple relationships.

IV. THREE ASSESSMENT TRACKS

Environment

The term ACA, in its broadest form, refers to the experience of growing up with an alcoholic parent(s). The environment refers to "what it was like": the experiences of daily, routine family life outlined by the popular press.

The alcoholic family has been described as chaotic, unpredictable, inconsistent, with arbitrary, repetitious and illogical thinking, and not infrequently violence and incest (Brown, 1988; 1991). There is an atmosphere of tension, fear and often pervasive shame (Brown, 1988). This is a family that is out of control, overtly or covertly, with no means to regain it.

Adjusting to the uncertainty of this kind of environment or "family context" requires enormous energy and attention. Children are forced to assume a reactive, defensive posture to accommodate to the reality of the drinking and the defensive maneuvers necessary to sustain it within the family.

In dealing with constantly changing standards of parental behavior and logic, chronic tension, and the unremitting potential for disaster, ACAs share a sense of being "on guard" as a lifestyle.

"The chaos was the only thing I knew for sure. I always could rely on the unexpected and the knowledge that I'd have to quickly adjust—turn my attention to the crisis at hand and get into gear. I always grew up on guard. It was the only way to survive."

"My mother's unpredictability was so distressing. I was always on guard and shielded from her violence and rage. I insulated myself emotionally and physically by just checking out. I don't know where I went mentally, but I sure left. Now I don't feel anything and I can't even remember much of what happened."

This guarded stance is described as a constant watchfulness, hyper-vigilance, and a defensive attitude of mistrust toward others. Because of the lack of basic environmental safety, children cannot feel secure and therefore free to focus their attention on their own internal development. Attention turns outward and self-development becomes dominated by the need for accommodation and defense. Several patients illustrate:

> *"I always expect a hostile environment. I see people as fierce, dangerous animals. I approach the world with suspicion and a belief that I will be betrayed and hurt."*

"Being on guard is what life is all about. I am always assessing the world around me—will I be trapped, make a mistake, break a rule and humiliate myself? Surviving means always staying one step ahead."

Trauma

Within the last few years, it has been widely accepted that the alcoholic home environment is "traumatic" (Cermak, 1986; Brown, 1988). Defined by psychiatrist, Henry Krystal (1978), trauma is the "overwhelming of the self's normal preservative function in the face of inevitable danger."

The "everyday" alcoholic environment or "life context" is likely to be characterized by what is called chronic or "strain" trauma, the chaos or inconsistency we've just seen in examples. Thus, what many kids experience as routine and normal, is also by definition traumatic. These same kids may also experience episodes of "acute" trauma that punctuate the "normal" atmosphere. Acute trauma might include a single experience, or many episodes of violence, incest, or a terrible fear coming home to an empty house. A child might also experience trauma through witnessing violence or abuse to others (Eth & Pynoos, 1985; van der Kolk, 1987). Many ACAs must struggle with survivor guilt because they escaped direct brutality when someone else did not.

The child's normal, natural mechanisms of defense and adaptation will be stretched to the limit. Eventually, children omit, redefine or distort information and affect in order to cope (Guidano & Liotti, 1983; Bowlby, 1988; Brown, 1988; 1991).

Reality can't be known. With this dominant emphasis on trauma and the constant need for defense, the child's basic sense of security is thwarted. Attention must go outward, with internal development impaired, arrested, or influenced and shaped by the dominance of environmental danger. The base of an "other-directed," reactive position in relation to others is firmly planted. So are the seeds for a fundamental mistrusting, guarded, insecure attitude toward others that will influence the subsequent development of the self and all interpersonal relationships.

The System

In shifting from the environment to systems theory, we move from what actually happened, what can be seen or not seen, and the way it feels, to a focus on how the family works, the mechanisms or structure that allow the alcoholic household to function.

Family systems theory explains how interactional patterns of relationship and behavior maintain a family's sense of balance, what is called technically, homeostasis or equilibrium (Bowen, 1974; Watzlavich, Weakland & Fisch, 1974; Satir, 1964). Homeostasis is a point of balance, not a judgment of health or well being. All groups, organizations, or families naturally strive toward achieving and maintaining a sense of internal stability.

The alcoholic family is a system dominated by alcohol, alcoholism, or the alcoholic as the central organizing principle, governing family dynamics and systems balance (Steinglass, 1980; Brown, 1977; 1985; 1988). The alcoholic family, contrary to popular belief (and inappropriate, incorrect popular terminology), is often a highly functional, but rigid and unhealthy system (Brown, 1991; Steinglass et al, 1987).

The family's dominant need for defense results in a tight, rigidly controlled, and narrow system. There are strict limits on behavior and what can be known and named. The realities of out-of-control behavior, tremendous cognitive and affective denial and distortion, and role confusion contribute to a rigidly regulated system with restricted access in and out (Steinglass et al, 1987; Guidano and Liotti, 1983; Brown, 1988). The alcoholic dominates the system, setting the shifting rules to which everyone else must adjust. The child's needs, feelings and behavior are subjugated to, and regulated by, the needs of the drinker.

How Does it Work?

John, an ACA in group therapy, recalled his childhood home and how the system worked:

> *"In my family alcohol was at the head of the table. My father's drinking organized our whole lives, but everyone would tell you that it wasn't true. My father was drunk every night, but no one could talk about what was happening. We all knew that Dad had a difficult job and drinking was his way of relaxing and giving him some relief from the stresses of work. In some way, we all believed that Dad was entitled to behave this way because of what he put up with every day and all he did for us."*

The alcoholic family becomes dominated by the presence of alcoholism and its denial as John illustrates. Maintaining this secret, the reality of alcoholism, while denying it at the same time, becomes the central double-bind focus around which family life is ordered.

Each individual develops the same behavioral and thinking disorder as the alcoholic: They are controlled by the reality of alcoholism and they must deny that reality at the same time. To preserve this inherent contradiction, all family members must adapt their thinking and behavior to fit the family's "story," that is, the explanations that have been constructed to allow the drinking behavior to be maintained and denied at the same time. The "story" includes core beliefs which family members share and which provide a sense of unity and cohesion, often against an outside world perceived as hostile or unsafe.

The strength of this systemic organizing principle is illustrated in family rules. One of our clients explained:

> *"There were two rules in our family: The first was 'there is no alcoholism' and the second was 'don't talk about it'."* (Beletsis & Brown, 1981)

Maintaining the unhealthy, pathological system requires a reactive stance and a dominant emphasis on accommodation and defense. What may be most visible and obvious, and is certainly most central, the drinking, is also most vehemently denied <u>and</u> explained as something else.

Why would anyone go along with this kind of blatant denial or even subtle distortion? We know from experts in child development (Kagan 1984; Miller, 1981; 1984) that all children need a very close human bond, what is called a primary attachment, in order to survive. Most often a parent fulfills this role. We also know that the preservation of this bond is of utmost importance to the developing child. Any threat or disruption in the parent-child bond will cause tremendous fear and anxiety in a child (Kagan, 1984; Lidz, 1973; Bowlby, 1980; 1985).

One of the greatest threats to family attachment and solidarity is the challenge of the family's denial about parental alcoholism. Children and adults will readily accept the secret keeping, joining the parents in the denial and distortion, in order to maintain family ties. Everyone in the family fears that telling the truth about drinking will result in loss of love, abandonment and perhaps the breakup of the family.

The realities of the traumatic out-of-control environment and the dominance of pathological systems dynamics take precedence over opportunities for healthy individual development. Indeed, one of the major consequences of family alcoholism is the sacrifice of healthy individual development to the greater need of maintaining the pathological system (Brown, 1988; 1991).

Individual Development

In addition to environmental and systems experiences, the term ACA also refers to individual development, the third assessment track. Clinical theory remains poorly articulated or understood in this domain with several exceptions (Wood, 1987; Beletsis and Brown, 1981; Brown, 1988; Brown, 1991). These authors have examined the developmental impact of parental alcoholism emphasizing the dominance of defense and necessity for accommodation to the demands of the environment, system and parental need. Attachment theory serves as an organizing construct that links these tracks and explains how individual development in an alcoholic family is grounded and organized around defense.

Attachment

Major developmental theorists including Jerome Kagan (1984), Margaret Mahler (1975), Eric Erickson (1963), Peter Blos (1962) and John Bowlby (1980; 1985; 1988) agree on the critical and fundamental importance of attachment to human development. Bowlby defines attachment as a very close tie with a care-giving or parental figure, usually the mother. No human being can survive without this kind of bond, the base on which all processes of normal childhood and adult development take place. This bond is so important that many difficulties and unhealthy adaptations in development can be traced to problems between parent and child or other significant figures such as siblings, grandparents, or other primary caretakers. Healthy development can also be explained on the basis of a strong, positive core attachment in infancy and the early childhood years.

There is virtually no argument that humans are social animals who develop and survive in relation to others. These core bonds are established and maintained throughout life by what Bowlby refers to as "attachment behavior," "any form of behavior that results in a person obtaining or maintaining proximity to some other clearly identified individual who is conceived as better able to cope with the world (Bowlby, 1988, p. 27)."

Bowlby suggests that attachment behavior is most obvious in early childhood, or when a person is frightened, fatigued or sick. An attachment figure provides comfort and care, giving the individual a strong feeling of security and therefore encouragement to value and continue the relationship (p. 27).

The origins of attachment theory lie with the neo-Freudians and later with the object-relations schools of individual development. The neo-Freudians, including Sullivan (1953), Horney (1937) and Fromm (1947), veered from the Freudian emphasis on intrapsychic drive, adding the critical shaping influence of interpersonal experiences in individual development. The object-relations school, represented by such early theorists as Winnicott (1953; 1960), Fairbairn (1952), and Guntrip (1969) elaborated the significance of interpersonal relationship to the development of the self. Most recently, the self-psychologists represented by Kohut

(1971) and others also emphasized the significance of core relationships to all individual development. The newest schools of cognitive-constructivism (Mahoney, 1977; Guidano and Liotti, 1983), control-mastery theory (Weiss and Sampson, 1986) and developmental psychopathology (Rolf et al, 1990) also stress the importance of the interpersonal bond and relationship patterns as developmental influences. These theorists accent the importance of deep beliefs a child develops about self and others in direct response to interactions with significant figures. These deep beliefs are often unconscious and enduring, serving as the organizing structure for perceiving and interpreting self and world. In this view, individuals develop certain core beliefs about themselves and the world based on early interactions. They then interpret self and world from a view that repeatedly reconfirms these basic beliefs regardless of their validity.

Attachment theory posits that the origins of the self—one's affective experience, identity, deepest beliefs, and patterns of relationship -- reside within the relationship of the child to its mother (or parent figure (Bowlby, 1980; 1988.) The child develops and internalizes core beliefs about the self and a persistent kind of relationship pattern that then serves as a model or template for all succeeding relationships.

Patterns of Attachment

Bowlby, in close collaboration with Ainsworth (Karen, 1990), defined three major patterns of attachment, each persistent over time between child and parent and later replicated with others in adult life. The first is a pattern of "secure" attachment in which the infant is confident that the parent (or parental figure) will be available, responsive, and helpful should painful or frightening situations arise. With assurance, the child feels confident in exploring the world. This pattern results when a mother is readily available, sensitive to the child's signals and responsive to the child's request for comfort and protection (Bowlby, 1988, p. 24). This pattern lays the groundwork for healthy development beginning with a close dependent bond that facilitates later emotional separation and autonomy.

The second pattern is "anxious resistant," in which the child is uncertain about the parent's availability or responsiveness. This uncertainty leads to separation anxiety and a tendency to be clinging and anxious about exploration. There is conflict in this pattern, reinforced by the uncertainty of the response and by threats of abandonment used as a method of control.

The third pattern is "anxious avoidant," in which the individual expects to be rebuffed when seeking care. Such individuals may attempt to become emotionally self-sufficient, living without the support and love of others. The traumatic alcoholic environment and pathogenic systems dynamics may both cause and/or reinforce anxious resistant or anxious avoidant patterns.

These patterns of attachment incorporate behavioral, cognitive and affective elements, and, like genetic coding, hold within them the most rudimentary early experiences with significant others and the most important feelings and beliefs about other people and the world.

Other theorists stress the importance of attachment and the problems in development related to the nature or pattern of this bond. Mahler (1975) suggested that the road to mature development starts with a very close dependent relationship, a "symbiotic" bond, in which parent and child are like one. This merged relationship and period of time in infancy correspond to what Erikson calls the first developmental stage of "basic trust." It is the infant's first experience with communication, the time when the child learns, through close contact with the mother or other primary care-giving figure, that he or she will be understood and responded to.

Or, as Alice Miller (1981; 1984) and others (Lidz, 1973; Winnicott, 1953;1965) suggest, the child learns the opposite: that parents cannot hear or respond because they are so dominated by their own problems, conflicts and needs. Miller describes a common but very unhealthy parent-child bond in which the child exists to reconfirm the parent's value or point of view and thus becomes an extension or tool of the parent. This is an insidious, often subtle kind of role reversal, in which the primary parent-child bond is structured to meet the needs and particularly the defenses of the parent rather than the child. This relationship structure leads to a loss of self, or the development of a "false self" (Winnicott, 1953; 1965) or a "defended self," in service to the parents, rather than healthy development and ultimate separation. This pattern also leads to an "anxious resistant" or "anxious avoidant" attachment pattern.

The alcoholic family is organized around the dominance and centrality of the traumatic, out-of-control environment, the rigid, defended system and the parents' predominant need for defense, which leads to a pattern of "reverse attachment" or role reversal as the predominant structure of the child-parent bond. A patient illustrates:

> "I was my mother's confidante from as early as I can remember. I had to listen, sympathize and offer suggestions that would somehow make everything O.K. But nothing ever changed. She was the child and I was the ineffective, helpless parent."

Most recently, developmental psychopathologists (Rolf et al, 1990) add to this picture, suggesting that children who must accommodate to parental need and defense as the context and structure for self development, may be characterized as "hard growing" or "straight jacket" survivors rather than resilient or "invulnerable" as previously believed. These theorists now suggest that the child's development is based on defensive adaptation, in response to the external demands of the environment, system and parental needs as a patient demonstrates:

> "Adjustment probably says it right, but I never knew that's what I was doing. I might have been mad if I'd have known. No, that's all there was. You just waited and watched, ready to swing this way or that to hold it all together."

Defensive Development

Bowlby and his colleagues accent the importance of open communication and accessibility between infant and mother. He, like classical theorists, and much like the interpersonal theorist, Harry Stack Sullivan, sees much of pathology as an over-emphasis on defensive processes. Sullivan believed that the core of unhealthy individual development rests on the assumption and solidification of a "fundamental malevolent attitude" (1953). The child experiences others and the world as anxiety-provoking and begins to enlist massive defensive operations to ward off the negative influence of others. As one patient told another:

"You are your defenses! We see, feel, and hear your barriers to the world, your rational processes, the way you keep people out, the way you explain, the way you defend yourself against enemies that aren't there now but certainly were there in your childhood."

The patient responded:

"I feel like a deck of cards: if you pull one out, the whole deck will collapse. I only exist as I am defending myself. Then I know that I am."

Bowlby (1980; 1985) and Sullivan (1953) suggest that a child shuts out, closes down, or otherwise does not see or take in information about others or the self that might threaten the parent or the all-important bond to the parent. Similarly, the child develops behaviors and affects consistent with the perceived needs of the parent and the overwhelming need to preserve the dynamics of the alcoholic family system.

Earlier (Brown, 1988) I spelled out an integrated theory based on the relationship between the central organizing influence of alcoholism in the environment, the family system and attachment. In that theory, I suggested that:

"Attachment -- early and ongoing -- is based on denial of perception which results in denial of affect which together result in developmental arrests or difficulties. The core beliefs and patterns of behavior formed to sustain attachment and denial within the family then structure subsequent development of the self including behavioral, cognitive, and affective development." (Brown, 1988)

In outlining the three assessment tracks, two factors stand out: first, the importance of the interpersonal perspective, organized by attachment theory, and second, the dominance of defense in accommodating to parental alcoholism. The environment is unsafe, the system is restrictive and pathological, and individual development is·characterized by unhealthy attachment patterns. Let us now move from the child to the adult and examine the impact of defensive development on interpersonal relationships. We will explore the dominance of defense within each assessment track and the fundamental interpersonal attitude, "relationship structure" or attachment pattern that results.

V.   INTERPERSONAL RELATIONS

> "Once upon a time everything was lovely, but that was before I had to deal with people." Harry Stack Sullivan (1953, p. 216.)

The Defensive Self in Adult Relationships

What do children of alcoholics bring to adult relationship? Adults born and raised in the environment, system and attachment patterns designed to sustain pathology experience the normal tasks and stages of close interpersonal development as threatening. They have internalized a sense of confusion, a requirement to "not know," the anxiety of the attachment bond and anxiety and fear about what relationship means. Physical and emotional safety and integrity are vested in the self. For many, being involved in a close, intimate relationship requires more defense, not less.

> "My whole sense of self is related to my ability to be self-sufficient, to defend against needing others or having others need me too much. You know what nurturance is? Nurturance is taking care of all of my own needs. Nurturance is successfully defending against closeness. Closeness means the loss of myself and destruction."

Another agreed:

> "A successful interaction means surviving without being humiliated, exposed, or revealing myself as bungling, starving, angry or overbearing. I end up in the delicate position of trying to balance superficial interactions to protect myself."

Nurturance—loosely, the feeling of being taken care of—is equated with surviving. It's a sense of relief, a feeling that one's defenses worked.

> "Nurturance means I win. I kept myself in control, intact, and didn't let others in. This is the only idea I have of being cared for. It comes only from me."

For these ACAs, relationship is toxic. For others, relationship holds a magical potential for fusion or rescue. These individuals maintain a hope of finding the idealized perfect mate, the one who will be the good parent, the adult needed early on. These ACAs feel lost, abandoned and orphaned as they suffer repeated disappointments in relationship. With either stance, intimate bonds are bound to bring up the need for defense so characteristic of childhood at all three levels.

The Environment

As we have seen, safety is chronically threatened for many children in alcoholic families. For others, safety is uncertain, regulated by parental drinking, inconsistency, unpredictability, and out-of control parental behavior. One's sense of self, view of others and basic framework of relationship are all structured by the level of physical and emotional safety and the need for defense. In emphasizing the interpersonal aspects of trauma, Krugman (1987) suggests that "avoidance of intimacy" or "relationship distortions" are also consequences. He emphasizes that "traumatic experience is central in organizing, structuring and reproducing the emotional, interpersonal, and systemic features common to abusive and intrusive families." (page 129.) He outlines specific consequences, accenting the dominance of defense, to avoid the recurrence of traumatic memory or experience. Unresolved, acute and chronic trauma "effects cognitive function, object relations, and interpersonal skills, leaving the victim with maladaptive first-order defenses, constricted ego function, and distorted role relationships." (p. 131.)

When trauma is chronic, it becomes normalized, more predictable, and easier to defend against. Yet the need for defense dominates; more and more of the self is organized to ward off vulnerability (p. 131).

Krugman further suggests that the defenses adapted by previously traumatized adults shape and limit the relationship structure of the couple and family they will form. He suggests that "trauma-driven deficits in cognitive, emotional, and interpersonal skills limit frustration tolerance, problem solving and conflict resolution." He adds that these families lack basic social skills, avoid anxiety-arousing situations, and often rely on drugs and alcohol. With poor boundaries and difficulties separating, they are likely to be socially isolated, psychologically impoverished, and vulnerable to stress of all kinds (p. 131).

Krugman also looks to Bowlby, suggesting that traumatized children will develop insecure attachments which then structure family relationships. The inconsistency of the parent-child relationship leads to anxiety over separation and abandonment alternating with avoidance of closeness and outright rejection. This anxiety regarding interpersonal closeness and distance matches what many describe as a central "co-dependence" problem, or disorder of relationship with ACAs -- the inability to find, create, or experience the "right amount" of intimacy with a partner.

> *"I'm always looking for the perfect person. I have this idea that if we're really a good match, really in love and in tune with each other, we should always know just what the other needs. But it doesn't happen. I'm always disappointed."*

The anxiety of the attachment bond also reduces the depth and breadth of the child's affective experience. In essence, children cannot have feelings about a reality that does not exist. They also cannot have perceptions that counter the explanations constructed by parents to protect themselves and the preservation of the drinking privilege.

Krugman (1987) describes several unhealthy patterns of trauma-driven relationship structures formed by adults who experienced childhood trauma and the anxious attachment believed to accompany it, including: 1) symbiotic fusion, the inability to experience or tolerate a sense of separate self; 2) re-enactment, replaying roles and relationship patterns from earlier experiences; or 3) disengagement, a distanced, controlled and often hostile relationship dominated by defense.

Trauma distorts internal models of object relationship. Parental relationships are often structured along dominant-submissive extremes. Models for identification are equally polarized. The child can identify with the aggressor, denying vulnerability, or with the victim, needing protection, but too frightened and untrusting to seek it or let it in.

Some individuals exposed to chronic trauma in the environment will develop an internal schema of chaos with trouble or crisis normative. These individuals may require constant stimulation to feel attached, "connected" or alive, at the same time they suffer continually from the pain of the trauma they now must create. Others may experience a different kind and level of trauma, living in an "anxious environment" characterized by fear and the constant potential for harm. These individuals may be more influenced by anxiety as an inherent feature of the interpersonal bond.

In this environment, the need to keep a secret and the ongoing threat of discovery mobilize defenses. Ultimately, the child shuts out, distorts and reinterprets reality. This massive closing down leads to chronic distrust of others, inhibition of curiosity, a distrust of one's own senses and a feeling that everything is unreal. A patient who grew up in an atmosphere of tension with frequent violence and chronic criticism describes his sense of awareness as an adult.

> *"I look at the world, people, events, and feelings through a filter. It's like a haze, a cheesecloth, that mutes the intensity of what's out there -- and what's coming in. I couldn't tolerate my feelings without this filter."*

ACAs may feel out of control in relationship. Polarized models ensure an unequal relationship structure. Mutuality, reciprocity, and flexibility in role -- characteristics of mature relationship -- are ruled out.

Close intimate adult bonds, organized by defensive needs and pathogenic internal models, often replicate the very childhood experiences or feelings they were designed to avoid.

The System

Alcoholic family systems dynamics are also predominantly defensive and reinforce unhealthy patterns of relationship. Interactional patterns, roles, beliefs, and behaviors are all structured to preserve the core pathology of the system.

> *The rigid, tightly regulated and increasingly defended alcoholic system (Steinglass et al, 1987) is characterized by disorders of hierarchy and boundaries (Krugman, 1987) and extremes of dominance and submission, a relationship structure necessary to sustain the pathology and a consequence of it. ACAs in treatment frequently recall the dictatorial nature of family relationships and family life.*

"There was one ruler, one king, and the rest of us were slaves. My father was the only one entitled to hold an opinion about anything."

Unhealthy systems dynamics are often reflected in role inconsistency and confusion between parents and in role reversal and triangulation between parents and children. Individual development is sacrificed to preserve the rigid, inflexible and increasingly threatened system.

ACAs experience great anxiety about all aspects of development, but it is particularly acute when it comes time to form their own intimate couple or family system. The paradigm for intimate relationship or family life dictates a loss of self to the preservation of a destructive, unhealthy "we." Many ACAs establish a comfortable adult life by ruling out close intimate bonds. As one patient put it:

"The only relationship is to be alone."

In the polarized system, there is a winner and a loser. This structure often guarantees an arrest in the developing couple relationship (Bader and Pearson, 1988). The couple cannot progress because one or both partners is bound to the unhealthy polarized structure of the first family. Loss of self, boundary diffusion and intrusion, fusion or disengagement are seen as normal. Within a structure that values the preservation of the system, or "we," autonomy <u>within</u> a close relationship will be viewed as selfish or rejecting.

Healthy relationship requires the ability to hold a strong "I" and a "we." With the polarized relationship structure of the alcoholic system, the flexibility required to maintain both perspectives is not possible. Individuals are stuck preserving a pathological "we," or defending an isolated, endangered "I."

The dominating power of unhealthy systems dynamics is reflected early in treatment as ACAs struggle with issues of guilt, betrayal and disloyalty implicit in accepting the label ACA and the need for help. For many, the very idea of autonomy or an identity separate from the family, is fraught with anxiety. As Shirley put it:

"If I even think about growing up, leaving home, and creating a family of my own, I'm overcome with guilt. Nobody ever leaves my family. We

learned one thing — the family is sacred. Nobody gets out and nobody gets in."

Individual Development

Given the dominance of trauma, systems pathology and parental need in structuring the attachment bond, children develop a sense of self dominated by a malevolent interpersonal attitude (Sullivan, 1953) and a strong need for defense. In essence, the "self"—that identity connected with "me" or "I"—is equated with the ability to successfully defend oneself.

> *"I have a deep sense of myself as needy and vulnerable, but I have an entirely different face I present to the world. The mask of competence, strength and defiance isn't real but I rely on it anyway. The facade is my bricks and mortar, my support of myself."*

Close adult partnerships will be formed from this base of a deeply vulnerable, needy, but "non-existent" or chronically endangered self, a self dominated by defense.

Another individual illustrates:

> *"I know at a deep level that I am needy, vulnerable, empty and sometimes non-existent. If I wasn't fending off, manipulating and constantly observing and taking in what's out there from a framework of danger and the need for protection, I wouldn't exist."*

From this deep view of the world and people as dangerous, the individual develops a constellation of defensive traits or maneuvers (Brown, 1988; 1991) that dominate all aspects of interpersonal relationship. These traits are designed to keep the enemy out, to minimize anxiety, fear and the threat of humiliation, experiences that characterize the anxious attachment with parents and the anxious, or angry, parental relationship pattern observed repeatedly by the child. These interpersonal defensive maneuvers include denial or perceptual and cognitive distortion, a need for control, all-or-none thinking and an overriding assumption of responsibility for others (Brown, 1988; 1991).

Denial

The child learns that denial preserves bonds, that reality is bound to and regulated by defensive need. The child's view of self and world is literally defined by the parents' needs at any given time. The child tacitly agrees to shut out, or redefine anything that might threaten the all-important bond to parents. In adult relationships, the individual shields out any threatening information and constructs a version of reality in response to the perceived dictates of the partner. This reinforces the submissive position, with all authority for the relationship vested in the other.

Alternatively, the individual denies and distorts by rejecting all perceived "demands" of the other. This more aggressive, often overtly hostile stance, declares the partner to be dangerous and the source of potential harm. This stance reproduces the anxious resistant or avoidant pattern often dominated by intense conflict in relationship.

Control

The dominance of defense also leads to an emphasis on control. The child experiences the absence of control in the environment and in the changing nature of reality. Basic survival becomes equated with the need for control of self and other. An adult patient illustrates:

> "*Everything is control. That's all there is. I need to be in control of myself, my perceptions, my feelings. I need to be in charge of my definition of reality. I need to control the distance between us, what and how much you say, feel or think. Close relationship means danger.*"

The dominant need to ward off anxiety and the chronic danger of calamity in relationship also result in an inordinate emphasis on control. It is sometimes experienced as a drive for perfection oneself, or a demand for rigid, strict "perfection" from others, which leads to chronic tension and anxiety (exactly what was to be avoided) in the relationship. The atmosphere is often one of "pins and needles." A patient illustrates:

> "*I can't do anything right. Anything out of place, any change in routine, any uncertainty about who does what leads to an outburst or outright tantrum.*"

This couple eventually could see that anything out of place instantly reminded Todd of his alcoholic home, particularly the chronic disarray, arguments and abuse that organized family life.

Todd's tantrums recreated the exact scenario modeled repeatedly by his parents—his mother could do no right and his father blew up.

All-or-None Thinking

Linked to control is the dominant cognitive-perceptual filter of all-or-none thinking, a concrete dichotomous frame that reduces all perception, cognitions and feelings to right or wrong, good or bad. The defensive emphasis on all three tracks restricts open, fluid, flexible thinking, while reinforcing rigid, rule-bound cognition, virtually eliminating tolerance for ambiguity, a hallmark of mature development and relationship.

In the all-or-none frame, individuals cannot hold conflicting thoughts or feelings at the same time. This set reinforces a restricted range of perception, cognition and affect in relationship and sustains the polarized, dominant-submissive, or victim-aggressor relationship structure.

This primitive thinking also characterizes the popular movement. Individuals who now identify with the "codependent" position in relationship may equate change or improvement with reversal — for example, "I used to be bad, but now it's you." In essence, the partners change position within the relationship structure but maintain the pathology.

Responsibility

Finally, defensive development is often structured by the as-sumption of responsibility. The child copes with the pathology of the environment, system and structure of relationship by develop-ing a view of self as bad, responsible for all that goes wrong. In Sullivan's view, the child takes on a "bad me" identity, versus the "good me" that stems from healthier interpersonal experiences or the "secure" attachment pattern of Bowlby. The "bad me" or "responsible me" is the natural result of role reversal, an attach-ment pattern that assigns responsibility for all aspects of parental welfare to the child.

The assumption of responsibility is also tied to omnipotence, a great protection for children who feel helpless, vulnerable and perhaps out of control themselves. Children who assume the identity of "bad me" maintain an idealized image of the parents instead of recognizing their incompetence and unavailability. All the problems then lie with the children whose task it is to fix themselves.

"I always knew deeply that I had caused all the pain. It had to be my fault. In a way, that was reassuring: if I caused the mess, then surely I could fix it too."

With an emphasis on defense and a deep, basic mistrust of others, the ACA is set to have troubles in a close couple relationship.

The ACA Couple

Recent theoretical advances in couple and family theory (Bader and Pearson, 1988; Steinglass, et al, 1987) emphasize development — the couple and family are not seen as static, but rather constantly in process, negotiating normal developmental tasks and stages leading to mature interpersonal relationships. Pathology results from arrest, restriction, or a dominance of defensive adaptation, the kind of defensive adjustment that characterizes adult children of alcoholics.

In Bader and Pearson's (1988) developmental model, the couple progresses normally through stages similar to those outlined by Mahler and others (1975) for the developing infant. The first stage is symbiosis, a healthy experience of close, fused bonding. In normal couple development, this intensity and merger do not last, although many couples see this fused partnership as ideal. Normal couple development moves toward differentiation as the partners begin to move away from the symbiotic fusion of their early bond. At this stage, they must learn to tolerate separateness and the emergence of a strong, healthy "I" in the relationship, while not losing the foundation of the "we."

The inability to tolerate differentiation leads to what is being called "codependence." Autonomy is sacrificed to preserve the system which then itself becomes unhealthy because it cannot grow.

The healthy couple moves on toward practicing, a time of greater distance and emphasis on individuation. Successful separation allows the couple to come back together in rapprochement. Here, there is flexibility, fluidity, and movement back and forth between the "I" and the "we".

The healthy couple in rapprochement, and the next and final stage of interdependence, has open access to all stages, tolerating the "regression" to the fused state and the moving away that naturally follows in the rhythm of healthy interdependence.

The couple in which one or both partners is ACA has trouble with close relationship to begin with. If the ACA can form a bond, the couple frequently gets stuck in the earliest stage, developing a closed, rigid and unhealthy symbiotic alliance. This partnership values merger, the avoidance of conflict and minimization of differences (Bader, 1990).

Alternatively, the ACA couple may form a "hostile-dependent" bond dominated by anger and conflict, in which the "I" is constantly endangered and therefore defended.

These relationship structures recreate the anxiety and chronic danger of the traumatic environment, the enmeshed or disengaged, polarized systems dynamics and the anxious attachment patterns of the earliest relationships.

The ACA suffers fears of abandonment and loss, while feeling chronic mistrust. Inconsistency and unpredictability may be recreated or warded off by rigid restrictions and limits. Any normal "coming and going" will be experienced as traumatic.

The ACA couple often gets stuck because differentiation, or the normal moving away process, is viewed as negative. A partner's need to separate within the relationship will be experienced as an abandonment, loss or betrayal. The move away automatically means "I did something wrong."

Or, the ACA feels needy and seeks close companionship, but mistrusts the other and expects to be disappointed, swallowed up or abused. The individual may challenge the partner constantly or move away sharply, denying any need. The couple develops a hostile-dependent bond in which the need is great but the anxiety more overwhelming.

The ACA cannot get out or get in — any move represents annihilation and loss, regardless of whether the individual is identified with the aggressor or victim. The ACA grew up with poor boundaries, difficulties separating from disturbed parents, social isolation, emotional impoverishment, and great vulnerability to stress. Forming a close relationship activates all of these problems.

ACAs may also have difficulties when their needs within the relationship differ. One partner may desire more autonomy than the other wants, or what the couple can accommodate. In this scenario, one partner is always feeling trapped and trying to "get more space" while the other just "wants to be close." Many couples never move beyond this stuck position of regulated distance based on apparently different needs.

Many ACA couples seek treatment because they are baffled and upset by their inability to create anything but a very troubled, defended or tightly restricted relationship. They have no internal schema for a healthy relationship.

Although their concept of relationship is based on survival and defense, they cannot comprehend why they keep repeating negative, defensive interaction patterns, or why they keep choosing the "wrong" partner, one who will only disappoint.

These ACAs enter relationships with a hope it will be different. But they also enter defended and proceed to recreate the trauma of the early family, the pathological systems dynamics and the anxiety of the early bond.

Or, they enter defended and closed, unconsciously frightened that intimate bonds will bring up a flood of intense feelings and memories from the past. They need and want a close partner, but are emotionally lifeless or inaccessible themselves. Many ACAs have cast off the capacity to feel as a protection and cannot reclaim it in the couple relationship. Or, they feel everything for everyone and are dominated by the need for control and over responsibility.

A patient in a long-term interactional therapy group for ACAs illustrates these numerous dilemmas for the defended ACA.

> "Toni is feeling anxious as she deepens her relationship. She can maintain a separate sense of herself and clear boundaries about what she sees, feels, and believes, but the clarity is brief. Then she feels herself sucked back into her old family system, now recreated with Jim. She wants to run away or she has to shut down emotionally to feel safe."

As Toni allows herself to feel close, she experiences painful and uncomfortable feelings that actually belong to childhood. Ironically, the closer she gets to Jim, the more defended she becomes. She sees that being close meant disaster in her family. Toni sees that the feelings of helplessness and fear, the "walking on eggs" with Jim, are feelings she must have experienced as a child. But the connection is still mystifying.

> "Toni feels a tremendous sense of guilt about becoming healthy herself and moving away from her early family. To move toward health means abandoning her family which will lead to their destruction."

Toni chuckled ironically: "The more progress I make, the more guilt I feel and the more defended I become."

VI. CONCLUSION: ACA: A RELATIONSHIP DISORDER OR DIAGNOSIS?

We began by challenging the concept of "codependence" and the move toward viewing ACA as an individual diagnosis. I proposed three major assessment tracks instead -- the environment, the system, and individual development perspectives -- to better deal with the complexity and the differences between ACAs. I proposed that the ACA develops a reactive, defended self which then influences the person's entire view of self, other and world. This dominance of defense has a particularly negative impact on the ACA's capacity and ability to form and sustain close intimate interpersonal relationships.

Are all ACAs disturbed? We do not know yet, and it certainly is too soon to draw such a conclusion. It may be true that all ACAs make defensive accommodations to parental alcoholism, but some also go on to form relationships in which their defenses work well or are complementary with those of a partner, just like non-ACA individuals. We may see that ACAs in treatment are the one's whose childhood accommodations and adult defenses are more restrictive than they are useful, also just like non-ACA individuals in treatment.

We might stretch, however, and say that the ACA develops an increasing vulnerability to anxiety in forming close bonds, based on the pathology of the early relationship structure on all three levels -- environmental, systems, and individual development. It may also be useful to speculate that the ACA develops a "state" disorder, similar to the "fundamental malevolent attitude" of Sullivan. The notion of "state" suggests a readiness or particular vulnerability to the defensive stance in relationship.

We should go no further. It is too soon to reduce the ACA "disturbance" to a "relationship disorder" or a diagnosis within the current DSM. With the multiple axes and multiple variables within each track, it is impossible and still undesirable to reduce the ACA experience to any single category or disorder.

This brings us full circle. The task for understanding the ACA is one of expansion. We need to add assessment tracks and all the infinite variety of variables necessary to improve our understanding of the commonalities of the ACA experience and the unique individual differences.

ACA REFERENCES

1. *Al-Anon Faces Alcoholism*. New York, Al-Anon Family Groups., 1984.

2. Bader, E. Personal Communication, 1990.

3. Bader, E. and Pearson, P. *In Quest of the Mythical Mate: A Developmental Model of the Couple Relationship.* New York, Brunner/ Mazel, 1988.

4. Beletsis, S. and Brown, S. A developmental framework for understanding adult children of alcoholics. Focus on Women: Journal of the Addictions and Health, 1981. Reprinted in: Brown, S., Beletsis, S. and Cermak, T. *Adult Children of Alcoholics in Treatment*. Orlando, Health Communications, 1989.

5. Black, C. *My Dad Loves Me, My Dad Has a Disease*. Denver, MAC, 1980.

6. Black, C. *It Will Never Happen to Me*. Denver, MAC. 1981.

7. Blos, P. *On Adolescence: A Psychoanalytic Interpretation*. New York, Free Press, 1962.

8. Bowen, M. Alcoholism as viewed through family systems theory and psychotherapy. Annals of the New York Academy of Science, 233, 115-122.

9. Bowlby, J. *Attachment and Loss*. Vol. 3. New York, Basic Books, 1980.

10. Bowlby, J. The role of childhood experience in cognitive disturbance. In: M. Mahoney and A. Freeman (Eds.), *Cognition and Psychotherapy*. New York, Plenum Press, 1985.

11. Bowlby, J. *A Secure Base*. New York, Basic Books, 1988.

12. Brown, S. Defining a Continuum of Recovery in Alcoholism. Doctoral Dissertation, California School of Professional Psychology, San Francisco, 1977.

13. Brown, S. *Treating the Alcoholic: A Developmental Model of Recovery.* New York, John Wiley and Sons, 1985.

14. Brown, S. Children with an alcoholic parent. In: N.J. Estes and M.E. Heinemann (Eds.), *Alcoholism: Development, Consequences and Interventions*. St. Louis, C.V. Mosby, 1986.

15. Brown, S. *Treating Adult Children of Alcoholics: A Developmental Perspective*. New York, John Wiley and Sons, 1988.

16. Brown, S. _Safe Passage: Recovery for Adult Children of Alcoholics._ New York, John Wiley and Sons, 1991.

17. Brown, S., Beletsis, S. and Cermak, T. _Adult Children of Alcoholics in Treatment_. Orlando, Health Communications, 1989.

18. Brown, S. and Beletsis, S. The Development of Family Transference in Groups for Adult Children of Alcoholics. International Journal of Group Psychotherapy, 97-114. Reprinted in: Brown, S., Beletsis, S. and Cermak, T. _Adult Children of Alcoholics in Treatment_. Orlando, Health Communications, 1989.

19. Brown, S. and Cermak, T. Group therapy with adult children of alcoholics. California Society for the Treatment of Alcoholism and Other Chemical Dependencies Newsletter. 7(7), 1979, 1-6.

20. Cermak, T. Children of alcoholics and the case for a new diagnosis of co-dependency. Alcohol, Health and Research World, 8, 38-42, 1984.

21. Cermak, T. _Diagnosing and Treating Co-Dependence_. Minneapolis, Johnson Institute, 1986.

22. Cermak, T. and Brown, S. Interactional group psychotherapy with the adult children of alcoholics. International Journal of Group Psychotherapy, 32, 375-389, 1982. Reprinted in: Brown, S., Beletsis, S. and Cermak, T. _Adult Children of Alcoholics in Treatment_. Orlando, Health Communications, 1989.

23. Diagnostic Criteria from DSM III-R. Washington D.C., American Psychiatric Association, 1987.

24. Erikson, E. _Childhood and Society_. New York, Norton. 1963.

25. Eth, S., and Pynoos, R. _Post-Traumatic Stress Disorder in Children._ Washington, D.C., American Psychiatric Press, 1985.

26. Fairbairn, W.R.D., _Psychoanalytic Studies of the Personality._ London, Tavistock Publications, 1952.

27. Fromm, E. _Escape from Freedom_. New York and Toronto, Farrar and Rinehart, 1947.

28. Guidano, V.F., and Liotti, G. _Cognitive Processes and Emotional Disorders._ New York, Guilford Press, 1983.

29. Guntrip, H. _Schizoid Phenomena, Object Relations and the Self._ New York, International Universities Press, 1969.

30. Horney, K. _The Neurotic Personality of Our Time._ New York, W.W. Norton, 1937.

31. Kagan, J. *The Nature of the Child*. New York, Basic Books, 1984.

32. Karen, R. Becoming attached. Atlantic, Feb. 1990, 35-70.

33. Kohut, H. *Analysis of the Self*. New York, International Universities Press, 1971.

34. Krugman, S. Trauma in the family: Perspectives on the intergenerational transmission of violence. In: B. van der Kolk, (Ed.), *Psychological Trauma*. Washington, D.C., 1987, 127-152.

35. Krystal, H. Trauma and affects. Psychoanalytic Study of the Child, 33, 81-116, 1978.

36. Lidz, T. *The Origins and Treatment of Schizophrenic Disorders*. New York, Basic Books, 1973.

37. Mahler, M., Pine, F., and Bergman, H. *The Psychological Birth of the Human Infant*. New York, Basic Books, 1975.

38. Mahoney, M. Reflections on the cognitive learning trend in psychotherapy. American Psychologist, 32(1), 5-13, 1977.

39. Miller, A. *The Drama of the Gifted Child*. New York, Basic Books, 1981.

40. Miller, A. *Thou Shalt Not Be Aware*. New York, Farrar, Straus, Giroux, 1984.

41. Newsweek, May, 1979, p. 79.

42. O'Neill, E. *Long Day's Journey Into Night*. New Haven, Yale University Press, 1955.

43. Satir, V. *Conjoint Family Therapy*. Palo Alto, Science and Behavior Books, 1964.

44. Steinglass, P. A life history model of the alcoholic family. Family Process, 19(3), 211-226, 1980.

45. Steinglass, P., Bennett, L., Wolin, S., and Reiss, D. *The Alcoholic Family*. Basic Books, 1987

46. Stern, D. *The Interpersonal World of the Infant*, New York, Basic Books, 1985.

47. Sullivan, H.S. *The Interpersonal Theory of Psychiatry*. New York, Norton, 1953.

48. Vaillant, G. and Milofsky, E. *Natural history of male alcoholism, IV. Paths to recovery*. Archives of General Psychiatry, 39(2), 127-133, 1982.

49. van der Kolk, B. <u>Psychological Trauma</u>. Washington D.C., American Psychiatric Press, 1987.

50. Vanicelli, M. <u>Group Psychotherapy with ACOA's</u>. New York, Guilford Press, 1989.

51. Watzlawick, P., Weakland, J., and Fisch, R. <u>Change</u>. Palo Alto, Science and Behavior Books, 1974.

52. Weiss, J. and Sampson, H. <u>The Psychoanalytic Process: Theory, Clinical Observation and Empirical Research.</u> New York, Guilford Press, 1986.

53. Wegsheider, S. <u>Another Chance: Hope and Health for the Alcoholic Family.</u> Palo Alto, Science and Behavior Books, 1981.

54. Winnicott, D.W., *Transitional objects and transitional phenomena*. International Journal of Psychoanalysis, 34, 89-97, 1953.

55. Winnicott, D.W., *The theory of the parent-infant relationship*. International Journal of Psychoanalysis, 41, 585-595, 1960.

56. Woititz, J. <u>Adult Children of Alcoholics</u>. Orlando, Health Communications, 1983.

57. Wood, B. <u>Children of Alcoholism: The Struggle for Self and Intimacy in Adult Life.</u> New York, New York University Press, 1987.

This paper was originally entitled "Codependence and ACAs: Theoretical expansion from an Interpersonal Perspective." It was presented at the National Consensus Symposium, Washington, D.C., October, 1991. Portions of this paper were used in an expanded article entitled "Alcoholism and Trauma: A Theoretical Overview and Comparison," published in the Journal of Psychoactive Drugs, 26(4), 1994. Portions of that paper appear in this monograph. Thay are reprinted with permission of the Journal of Psychoactive Drugs. All rights reserved.

A Methodology and Current Estimate of the Number of Children of Alcoholics in the United States

Lewis D. Eigen, Ed.D. & David W. Rowden, Ph.D.

Introduction

In 1982 a study was conducted for the State of New York which estimated that in 1980 there were one half million children of alcoholics (COAs) in New York and 5.5 million in the United States.[1] Essentially the methodology utilized was to start with the number of adult "alcoholics" in the nation and extrapolate to the number of children under 20 by using the ratio of adults to children in the general population.[2] The methodology was based on an earlier study which estimated the number of COAs for the State of Pennsylvania.[3] In 1982 the estimate of adult alcoholics that was available to the researchers was crude at best, and the researchers did the best[4] that they could with the data and information that was then available. In 1985 the same general methodology was again used[5], this time with 1979 prevalence estimates based upon more than "guesstimates."[6] The number of COAs for the United States was estimated to be 6.6 million. This estimate was considerably larger (20%) than that of the 1982 study. The difference was more striking when one considers that the researchers changed the age definition for COAs to include only those youngsters under the age of 18, rather than the 20 year criterion that had been utilized earlier. The marked increase in COAs was far greater than what could be explained by demographic changes and was almost certainly due to a better prevalence estimate.

Subsequent to these efforts, there has been a substantial leap forward in the epidemiology of alcohol usage and alcoholism. In addition, the demographics of the U. S. population have changed considerably since then. However, heretofore, there have been no new studies estimating the number of COAs. Also, much more is known today about the additional risks to which COAs are exposed.[7] Many private and public agencies are developing policies and programs for protecting COAs and/or ameliorating the problems caused by additional risk factors. To plan, fund and/or implement these policies and programs, reasonable quantitative estimates of the number of COAs are required.

It is the purpose of this paper to produce such contemporary COA estimates. The plural is utilized because the COA estimate is fundamentally dependent upon two definitional issues: the definition of an alcoholic, and the definition of a child of an alcoholic. As this paper will articulate, there are several reasonable definitions of each of these elements, and each produces a somewhat different COA estimate. Therefore, this paper will articulate a methodology and calculate different definitions dependent upon which definitional assumptions are made. It is important to note, however, that under all definitional possibilities, the current estimates are considerably higher than those obtained in the 1982 and 1985 studies. Some of the methodological reasons for these differences will also be discussed.

COA Alternative Concepts

When we speak of the child of an alcoholic, the purpose is generally to examine the risk factors to the child and/or the actions that might be taken to prevent or reduce those risks. When we think of COAs, we might have any of the following concepts in mind.

I.   Children whose biological parents are or have been alcoholics.[8]
II. Children who are currently living with alcoholic parents or caregivers.
III. Children who have ever lived with alcoholic parents or caregivers.

These are not mutually exclusive of course. Many children in today's complex society do not live with both biological parents, and some live with neither biological parent. The presumption is that there is a statistical and likely causal relationship between the well-being and development of the child and the parent's or caregiver's problems with alcohol. The linkage might be hereditary, behavioral, cultural or some combination of these. Therefore, if the purpose of estimating the number of COAs is to estimate the number of children potentially at additional risk, then we should be estimating the number of children in any one or any combination of factors of I, II or III since each are capable of producing risk.

The following example illustrates the complexity:

Neither biological parent is alcoholic, but parents are divorced and remarried. The step-parent of the children living in the home of the custodial, natural parent has an alcohol problem.

In the modern, nuclear family, the addition of step-parents or parent surrogates adds significantly to the risk likelihood from non-hereditary factors and adds to the COA estimate. Although the methodology developed and utilized in this paper will allow this type of analysis, the remainder of this paper will confine itself to the COA risk of the biological parents only. Thus all estimates herein will be conservative in this sense. A later analysis in another study will deal with estimates of additional risk if parent surrogates are included as well.

For a COA estimate there are three distinct types of COAs that could be defined. They are:

COCAs: **C**hildren **O**f **C**urrent **A**lcoholics

This includes those children whose parents would be classified as "alcoholic" sometime in a particular year. Excluded would be children, whose parents might have been drinking alcoholics in the previous year or earlier but were no longer so. This is a much more restrictive definition of a COA than were used in the text of the 1982 and 1985 studies where the issue of current, lifetime or parental period prevalence was not directly addressed.

COPPAs: **C**hildren **O**f **P**arental **P**eriod **A**lcoholics

If we are interested in children under the age of 18, there is an 18 year "parental period" during which the child could be exposed to risk from an alcoholic parent. Therefore, an 18 year parental period prevalence of alcohol problem period would define this category. The parent of a COPPA may have been a drinking alcoholic for a single short period during the 18 year parental period or the parent may be classified as an alcoholic for the entire 18 year period or anything in between. Note that the COPPA definition, like the COCA definition, precludes the risk of problem transmitted from parents who may have been alcoholics prior to the birth of the child. Thus, both of these will not account for the risk of genetic effects, Fetal Alcohol Syndrome (FAS) or Fetal

Alcohol Effects (FAE), for those children of parents who are in recovery.

COLAs: Children Of Lifetime Alcoholics

Here the child may have a parent who was **ever** a drinking alcoholic. This includes not only the parental period, but also the period before the child was ever born. To the degree that pharma-cological and genetic factors transmit additional risk, this COLA definition is critical in that COPPA and COCA definitions would completely ignore this factor, unless the parental problem also manifested itself at some time in the child's developmental years. Also, there are many who believe that there are often dysfunc-tional behavioral influences on children of sober adult alcoholics in recovery even if they have been abstinent for years.

It follows, therefore, that all COCAs are also COPPAs, and likewise all COPPAs are also COLAs. From a mathematical point of view,

$$\# \; COLAs \; > \; \# \; COPPAs \; > \; \# \; COCAs$$

This study attempts to provide national estimates for all three definitions. COAs under 18 years of age are considered, as in the 1985 study, rather than under 20 as had been done in the 1982 study. The reasons are several fold. First, 18 has become the age of majority in all states. In addition, many governmental programs directed at children do not apply to young people over the age of 18. It is noteworthy that even with the markedly more narrow definition of child, the COA estimates that are produced herein are considerably larger than the earlier estimates using the 20 year old criterion.

Alcoholism Prevalence

In order to estimate the number of children of alcoholics, one must first have an estimation of the number of alcoholics them-selves. There has been much debate over the various possible definitions that could be used to make such an estimate, and it has even been argued that there is no discrete point at which drinkers become alcoholics–that there is a continuum, and that the very concept of an alcoholic is based on a false premise of non-continuity[9]. In the 1982 study the words "alcoholics," "alcoholic homes," "problem drinkers," and "problems in drinking behavior" are utilized somewhat interchangeably. The common thread was to estimate the prevalence of a condition that exposes children to additional health risk.

Recent attempts at measuring alcoholism prevalence center around utilization of the DSM-III and DSM-III-R diagnostic criteria, and estimates of "alcoholics" proceed from that.[10] In this methodology we build upon the seminal surveys conducted by NIAAA utilizing the DSM-III definitions. These are criteria for establishing medical diagnostic conditions. For purposes of determining alcoholism prevalence to estimate the number of children of alcoholics, we used the DSM-III-R criteria for *alcohol dependence* and for *alcohol abuse*. Either condition in a parent[11] may produce the kinds of additional risk factors that COA investigations indicate.[12] It has been argued by some that the definition of alcoholic should be limited to *alcohol dependence* and should not necessarily include *abuse* in the absence of *dependence*. While we have accepted the "either/or" NIAAA definition, we observe that had the alternative been chosen, all estimates herein would have been somewhat reduced.[13] Further, that others using the data of this study be particularly careful in extrapolations of findings to other studies where the alternative definition of alcoholic (or even another definition) might have been utilized.

The most recent and comprehensive estimates have been given by NIAAA as a result of the 1988 NHIS survey. This study estimates the annual prevalence of "alcohol dependence" and "alcohol abuse." But one of the thorniest issues in estimating the number of COAs is which prevalence to use for the definition of parental alcohol problem. Monthly prevalence? Weekly? Yearly? Lifetime prevalence? The answer, of course, depends on the COA definition chosen: COLA, COPPA or COCA.

Since the COA concept involves the risk of influence of parents with alcohol problems, annual (or less) prevalence **underestimates** the number of COLAs or COPPAs. A parental alcohol problem, which may not have existed through the first 8 years of a child's life, may be present for the next 10 years or vice versa. Even if a parental alcohol problem existed before the birth of a child and not after, there is still the possibility that genetic or other familial/social influences might affect the child. However, a lifetime prevalence would overestimate the appropriate prevalence for all three of our definitions since it would include those parents who had alcohol problems **only after** the children were grown. The point is somewhat moot in that there are no reliable studies of lifetime prevalence of DSM-III-R diagnoses. What ideally is needed is a concept of **parental age prevalence**–the lifetime prevalence of the parent **only** up to the point that the children are no longer children, which for this purpose we will consider to be 18 years. So the **parental age prevalence is clearly *less* than lifetime prevalence but *greater* than annual prevalence**. If a parental age prevalence were known, it would be ideal for calculating the number of COLAs. Then if a pre-parental age prevalence could be calculated (the lifetime prevalence of the parent up to the point at which the child is born), then there would be a sound prevalence estimate for using the COPPA definition – namely, subtracting the pre-parental age prevalence from the parental age prevalence. There are no known, national, direct studies of parental age prevalence or pre-parental age prevalence, as there are none of lifetime prevalence, but there are ways of making reasonable estimates.

COLA Estimate

The COLA estimate is the easiest of the three definitional estimates to obtain. The methodology proposed in this study, regardless of COA definition, involves three distinct steps. First, is obtaining the appropriate estimate of the prevalence that matches the COA definition. Second, is utilizing that prevalence to calculate the *COA probability*, the likelihood that a particular child would have an alcoholic parent. And third, applying the COA probability to the demographics of the nation (or subdivision thereof.)

Table 1 shows the annual prevalence rates for the different age groups for "alcohol dependence," or "alcohol abuse," as estimated by NIAAA in 1988.

Table 1
Annual 1988 Prevalence of DSM-III-R Alcohol
Abuse or Dependence[14]

Sex	Ages 18-29	Ages 30-44	Ages 45-64	Age 65 +
Male	23.50%	14.30%	7.24%	2.77%
Female	10.10%	4.07%	1.73%	0.37%

For the COLA definition, we would want a lifetime prevalence rate for the parent up to the parental age when the child becomes 18. Since it is rare that a person over the age of 65 would have a child under 18, a 0-64 year parental prevalence would be appropriate. There is no such measure available from the NIAAA survey or anywhere else. However, the annual prevalence for each of the age groupings under 65 is always a lower bound of the 0-64 year prevalence. For each sex there are three annual prevalence figures (depending on age group under 65), and the maximum becomes the greatest lower bound for the 0-64 prevalence. For males, this is 23.50%, and for females, 10.10%[15]. Utilization of these prevalence rates will be a very conservative technique in that they **always underestimate** the 0-64 prevalence rate. This concludes step 1 for COLAs.

Estimating the COA Probability

Previous attempts to calculate the number of COAs from adult prevalence rates utilized methods of extrapolating the ratio of children to adults from the general population to the sub-population of alcoholics.[16]

There is an alternative and somewhat simpler and straight forward method of estimating the number of COAs given the alcoholism prevalence rates. Specifically, every child has both a male and female parent. Straight probability analysis can be used to answer the relatively simple question: *What is the probability that, for a particular child, at least one of the two parents is an alcoholic?* Essentially we call this the *COA probability.* If the male and female prevalence rates are P_m and P_f respectively, then the probability for a particular child would be given by:

$$P_{coa} = P_m + P_f - P_m P_f$$

But this assumes that P_m and P_f are independent – that the likelihood that an alcoholic would marry and/or have a child with another alcoholic is no different from chance. This assumption is certainly not tenable, given the well established cultural set of influences on both marriage and drinking patterns. If the probability that a particular alcoholic female would marry an alcoholic male were simply random, it would be the male prevalence, P_m. Clearly, it is higher than that, however. If it were given by M, then

$$P_{coa} = P_m + P_f - MP_f$$
Since $M > P_m$, then $(P_m + P_f - MP_f) < (P_m + P_f - P_mP_f)$

In the most extreme case **all** female alcoholics could be assumed to marry male alcoholics and therefore $M = 1$. Then

$$P_{coa} = P_m + P_f - MP_f \text{ or simply}$$
$$P_{coa} = P_m$$

Therefore an upper bound for Pcoa would be
$$P_m + P_f - P_mP_f$$
and a lower bound would be given by P_m.

Utilization of the lower bound would be a very conservative process and would always somewhat underestimate the actual number of COLAs. However, as will be seen, even utilizing this lower bound, the estimates are considerably higher than previous estimations.

Since for the COLA definition, $P_m = .235$ and $P_f = .101$,
$$.235 < P_{coa} < .235 + .101 - (.235)(.101), \text{ or}$$
$$.235 < P_{coa} < .312$$

The COLA Estimate

In 1988 there were 63.8 million children under 18 years of age in the United States.[17] Utilizing the COA probability range for COLAs just computed, the envelope of COLAs in the United States in 1988 was
$$15.0 \text{ million} < \# \text{ COLAs} < 19.9 \text{ million}$$

The difference between the 15.0 million estimate and the 19.9 million estimate lies in the proportion of female alcoholics who bear children fathered by male alcoholics. The 15.0 million number assumes all of them do, and the 19.9 million assumes that a female alcoholic is no more likely to have a child sired by a male alcoholic than any other woman. Reality lies somewhere in between.

COPPA Estimate

A similar process can be followed to obtain the COPPA estimate except that the prevalence rate is different. The highest male prevalence rate as shown in Table 1 is for the 18 to 29 year age group. That prevalence was appropriate for COLA estimates but for COPPA estimation, the 23.50% prevalence is only appropriate for those males who father their children before the age of 30. Therefore, what is needed for the COPPA estimate is an age prevalence weighted by the proportion of children fathered at the different age ranges. Fortunately, data to produce such a weighting is available. Figure 1 shows the male fertility by age of father. Table 2, which is derived from the Figure 1 fertility data, shows the proportion of children that are fathered by men in the same age ranges as is used by NIAAA in the DSM-III-R 1988 prevalence analysis.

Figure 1 Male Fertility Rate[18] (Births per 10,000)

Table 2
Percentage of Children Fathered By Men of Different Ages[19]

	Ages 18-29	Ages 30-44	Ages 45-64	Age 65+
% of Children Fathered	53.3%	41.2%	2.6%	0

If the male prevalence rates are weighted proportionately the combined rate is 18.6%. And if the same proportions are applied to the female rate, it is 8.0%. This process assumes that the fertility rates for both male and female alcoholics are not substantially different from those of their non-alcoholic age counterparts.[20] Therefore, for calculating the COA probability for COPPAs, P_m = .186 and P_f = .080. When these numbers are applied,

$$.186 < P_{coa} < .186 + .080 - (.186)(.080), \text{ or}$$
$$.186 < P_{coa} < 0.251$$

This in turn, when applied to the 63.8 million children under 18 years of age, produces

$$11.9 \text{ million} < \text{\# COPPAs} < 16 \text{ million}$$

Just like the COLA estimates, the difference between the ends of the range are a function of the alcoholic male/female marriage and breeding pattern. Also, the conservative nature of dealing with the prevalence issue assures that the range itself is an underestimate of the true number, just like the COLA estimate, in that an average, weighted, annual prevalence was utilized rather than a multi-year prevalence for the 18 year COCA exposure period.

COCA Estimate

In the COLA and COPPA estimating procedure previously described, we chose lower bound estimates of prevalence by utilizing the annual prevalence survey by NIAAA. Ideally we would not have utilized annual prevalence which underestimates the results. However, for the COCA estimate we do want the actual annual prevalence. The problem is that the NIAAA data present average prevalence figures by age group and for the population as a whole, but what is needed for the COCA estimate is a prevalence weighted for the parental period only – not the general population prevalence. This is not immediately available from the NIAAA data, but can be reasonably estimated.

Figure 2
% of Children Born By Paternal Age

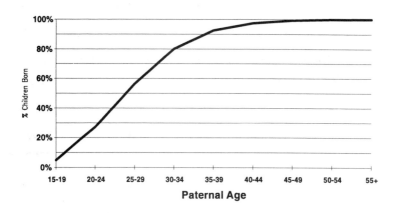

The data from Figure 2 demonstrate that 28 years is currently the approximate, median age of paternity in America. Also, that over 97% of the children are born before the father has reached the age of 45. Extending this by the 18 year parental period essentially means that only 3% of the fathers ever reach the age of 65 during the parental period. Likewise, approximately only 50% even reach the age of 45 during the parental period. There-fore, when weighting the COCA paternal prevalence, we should eliminate 97% of the over 65 population and 50% of the over 45 group. Likewise, 44% of the males under the age of 29 have not yet fathered a child; nor have 3% of those men under the age of 44. Therefore, equivalent proportions of these age groups should be ignored for weighting purposes. Table 3 shows the figures utilized for the male weighting procedure.

After adjusting the weighting for these removals, the weighted, male, annual prevalence rate is 15.05%.

Table 3
Weighting for Males (in Millions)

	Age 18-29	Age 30-44	Age 45-64	Age 65+	Total
Male Population	24,677	28,441	22,042	12,355	87,515
Proportion Included	53.30%	100.00%	50.00%	2.60%	
Prevalence	23.50%	14.30%	7.24%	2.77%	**15.05%**
Population Included	13,153	28,441	11,021	321	52,936
Alcoholics Included	3,091	4,067	798	9	7,965

If a similar weighting system is utilized for females, there will be a slight underestimate of the proper prevalence in that females marry and become parents at a slightly earlier age than the males. However, the error thus induced is relatively small, and the COA probability estimate is much more heavily controlled by the male rate than the female anyway.[21] Table 4 shows the parallel weighting for females.

The female weighted prevalence rate is, by this analysis, 4.96%.

Table 4
Weighting for Females (in Millions)

	Age 18-29	Age 30-44	Age 45-64	Age 65+	Total
Female Population	24,239	28,779	22,843	18,018	94,897
Proportion Included	53.30%	100.00%	50.00%	2.60%	
Prevalence	10.10%	4.07%	1.73%	0.37%	**4.96%**
Population Included	12,919	28,779	11,922	468	54,088
Alcoholics Included	1,305	1,171	206	2	2,684

Therefore, for calculating the COA probability for COCAs, P_m = .1505 and P_f = .0496. When these numbers are applied,

$$.1515 < P_{coa} < .1515 + .0496 - (.1515)(.0496), \text{ or}$$
$$.1515 < P_{coa} < 0.1936$$

This in turn, when applied to the 63.8 million children under 18 years of age produces

$$9.66 \text{ million} < \# \text{COCAs} < 12.35 \text{ million}$$

COA Estimate Summary

Thus far, we have produced a range for each of the three COA definitions. Where in the range the best estimate falls is a function of the intra-alcoholic childbearing and marriage patterns. There is insufficient knowledge at this time to know with any degree of certainty what the M value should be to make an ideal estimate.[22] However, it is not unreasonable to assume a value of .5. This would mean that one half of the alcoholic women who bear children would have done so with an alcoholic man. If it were left completely to chance, the proportion would equal the male prevalence rate. As can be seen in Table 1, the assumption that M = .5 would indicate that the intra-alcoholic breeding pattern was over 2 to 3 times greater than chance for the high fertility ages. The lower bound assumes that all female alcoholics interbreed with male alcoholics, while the upper bound assumes that the inter-breeding is completely random–an equally unrealistic assumption in the other direction. Table 5 provides all these estimates.

Table 5
COA Estimates (in Millions)

	Lower Bound M = 1	Estimate M = .5	Upper Bound Random
COCA	9.6	11.0	12.4
COPPA	11.9	14.0	16.0
COLA	15.0	17.5	19.9

Table 6
COA Estimates as a Percentage of the Youth Population

	Lower Bound $M = 1$	Estimate $M = .5$	Upper Bound *Random*
COCA	15%	17%	19%
COPPA	19%	22%	25%
COLA	24%	27%	31%

Therefore, we believe that the best estimates that can be given at this time are:

There are 11 million COCAs in the United States, 14 million COPPAs and 17.5 million COLAs.

17% of our youth are COCAs, 22% are COPPAs, and 27% are COLAs.

Differences From Earlier Estimates

The estimates obtained in this study are substantially higher than those obtained in the 1982 and 1985 studies. This is especially dramatic in light of the fact that the methodology utilized herein underestimates for the COLA and the COPPA definitions. There are several possible reasons for this apparent discrepancy. What might be thought to be one of the apparent factors, a demographic change in the number of children, is not a factor. As a matter of fact, the number of children under the age of 18 actually decreased from 1980 to 1988–to 63.8 million. There are several factors however that do account for most of the differences.

Age Definition Change

Some difference is due to the fact that the 1982 study counted children up to age 20 while the 1985 and this study limits the COAs to children under the age of 18.

Ratio of Adults to Children

Both the 1982 and 1985 studies utilized the approach, developed by Booz-Allen in the 1974 study, of calculating the ratio of adults to children and applying this ratio to the number of adult alcoholics estimated for the population as a whole. This methodological approach, while seemingly appropriate in the abstract, always seriously underestimates the number of COAs. The reason lies with the alcohol and fertility characteristics of the older people in our society. Alcoholism prevalence decreases markedly for both sexes as age increases. At the same time, very few older Americans are in a position to any longer influence the behavior of their children under 18 (or 20 as in the 1982 study). This is not to say that they are not influential. Their children are usually grown and are no longer under 18. They cannot influence a child who would be counted as a COA only because the child has passed the critical age. The overwhelming majority of children (over 97%) are born to parents under 46 years of age. Thus, there are only a minuscule handful of children under 18 with parents over 65. In using the ratio method, these mature adults were counted in the pool of adults. They, however, no longer can affect any of the factors impinging on children under 18 since their children have already passed that age. They also add very little to the number of DSM-M-R alcoholics since the over 65 prevalence is so low. By being included in the sample, they increase the ratio that is utilized but are neither parents nor alcoholics to any great extent. Therefore, they artificially decrease the Booz-Allen method, ratio derived estimates. In 1980 there were 25.5 million Americans 65 years or older, and this represents about 16% of all the adults over the age of 18 (an even greater proportion of those over 20.) Conceptually, they should be removed from the ratio calculation, and their contribution to the number of alcoholics should likewise be removed. The former is very large, while the latter is very small. The result of not doing so is to deflate the COA estimate. A rough calculation of this type was performed on the 1985 study data (data for 1980), and it showed that the over 65 factor alone accounted for an underestimate of about 20%. It is worth noting that by 1988, the over 65 year proportion of the adult population had increased significantly over 1980, and therefore, this underestimate increases in proportion and magnitude as the proportion of mature Americans increases in the population as a whole.

The same principle should be applied to the over 45 year old group as well. For the 45 to 65 year age group as parents, **approximately half** of their children have already passed 18. And, while the DSM-111-R alcoholism prevalence for this range is not as low as the over 65 group, it is lower than the average for the younger, parental period age groups. If half of this population were removed from the ratio, along with the corresponding reduction in the number of adult alcoholics, there would be far more COAs added to the estimate. So the Booz-Allen ratio method alone causes a substantial undercount of COAs.

Prevalence Estimates

It is certainly the case, as the authors acknowledge, that the 1982 study had little more of an alcoholism prevalence estimate than a "guesstimate." The 1985 study had a better estimate. In this study, we had the advantage of utilizing the results of NIAAA's substantial biometry efforts of the last few years. It is more than likely that these different prevalence estimates may have accounted for a substantial part of the estimation difference between this study and the two earlier ones.

Prevalence Period

In both the 1982 and 1985 study reports, the authors clearly indicate that they were concerned with congenital factors, FAS, FAE, cultural influences and the like. Although they do not explicitly distinguish among the COLAs, COPPAs and COCAs, the language of the reports indicated that these researchers had a COLA concept in mind. Yet the prevalence figures they had to work with were only annual prevalence figures. So, while they were likely thinking COLA, or certainly COPPA, they were actually calculating COCA and as we have already shown,

$$\text{\# COLAs} > \text{\# COPPAs} > \text{\# COCAs}$$

and this inevitably led to an underestimate.

Psychological / Political Factors

The 1985 study was performed by individuals who were among

the earliest leaders in bringing the attention of the nation, in general, and the health establishment, in particular, to the nature and implications of the COA problem. Their work was supported by the Children of Alcoholics Foundation which was not an entirely disinterested party. At the same time, there was not the national recognition of the COA problem that there is today. It is possible that the researchers and the COA Foundation "bent over backwards," as it were, to avoid being "alarmist" or appearing to exaggerate the magnitude of the problem. The methodology that was chosen, at each step, would underestimate rather than overestimate. The number of children at risk that were estimated was already, clearly, a serious problem of national significance, and there may have been great reluctance to utilize more complex, less traditional methodology or innovative methodology which would increase the estimate, lest they be accused of trying to magnify the problem. In particular, the choice to use the Booz-Allen ratio method, the only published method in the literature at that time, virtually guaranteed a substantial undercount.

In a sense, we have also been somewhat conservative, only to a lesser extent. We have chosen lower bounds throughout, so that to the degree there is error in the methodology, it is on the side of caution and underestimation.

Recent Parallel Results

Recently, the National Center for Health Statistics has reported an analysis of the 1988 NHIS national survey data in which over 40,000 Americans were asked whether they grew up in a household with a parent who was an alcoholic.[23] This survey was not designed to project the number of COAs and had other purposes driving the design and instrument. It only queried adults—not children under the age of 18. Further, the survey depended on self-definition and subjective perception, with the concomitant risk of denial or exaggeration and memory problems of the respondent in terms of whether the parent was an alcoholic, as opposed to some more objective measure such as DSM-III-R. This survey produced an 18.1% prevalence estimate for current adults who report growing up in alcoholic homes. If this proportion were extrapolated downward to the 1988 under 18 year old population of 63.8 million, the estimate of children would be approximately 11.5 million. This estimate, produced by a much different methodology with different definitional criteria as well, is much larger than the estimates of the 1982 and 1985 studies. It is right in the middle of our COCA estimate range as given in Table 5 and somewhat less than our COLA and COPPA estimates. The latter, in particular, is conceptually closer to the questions as posed to the survey recipients. Therefore, this study would support the contention that the 1982 and 1985 studies were underestimates, but would not suggest the same size underestimate as our study did.

Implications

There are certainly enough COAs in the nation, even under the 1982 and 1985 estimates, to constitute a major public health problem. The fact that there are many more than previously thought does not change the fundamental fact that there are children at risk. However, in addition to the academic exercise of having more precise estimates, there are major public policy implications of the difference in order of magnitude of the problem. To the degree that COAs require more educational, social or medical costs to the society, the number of COAs who could potentially benefit from programs is an important factor in making cost-benefit analyses of different prevention and intervention strategies. Such analyses and extrapolations should be performed with great care, however. In studies heretofore there has been relatively little attention paid to the possible range of COA definitions as well as different definitions of "alcoholics." In a health cost study, for example, it is possible that the higher medical costs of COAs applies disproportionately less to COLAs than to COCAs, or to either differentially to the COAs utilizing the definition in that study. It is, therefore, recommended that future studies involving COAs try, to the extent possible, to be as precise as possible, not only in involving COLAs, COPPAs or COCAs, but also in using DSM-III-R definitions of "alcoholics."

Given the broadest COA definition, the COLA estimates herein, one in four American children is at additional, potentially preventable, health risk. And under the most narrow definition, COCA, almost one in five children has a parent who is a drinking alcoholic which poses an increased health risk. The consequences of that additional risk, while primarily borne by the children themselves, impact every American, fiscally and otherwise.

Notes

*This study was performed pursuant to Contract #277-90-4002 of the Center for Substance Abuse Prevention, SAMHSA, Public Health Service of the U. S. Department of Health and Human Services. The authors wish to acknowledge the assistance of Dr. Bridgit Grant of NIAAA, Ms. Judi Funkhouser of the Center for Substance Abuse Prevention, Mr. George Marcelle of Social and Health Services Ltd, Ms. Migs Woodside, Dr. Sheila Blume and Mr. Basil Henderson of the National Foundation for the Children of Alcoholics, and Ms. Lynn Hadley, Ms. Cathy Crowley and Ms. Peggy Williams of the National Clearinghouse for Alcohol and Drug Information whose invaluable assistance in this endeavor is gratefully acknowledged.

1   Migs Woodside, Children of Alcoholics: A Report to Hugh L. Carey, Governor, State of New York, New York State Division of Alcoholism and Alcohol Abuse, 1982.

2   In 1980, this ratio was 1.8 for the nation and 2.3 for New York.

3   Booz-Allen and Hamilton, Incorporated, An Assessment of the Needs of and Resources for Children of Alcoholic Parents, National Institute on Alcohol Abuse and Alcoholism, 1974. This study utilized a 14 million national estimate of alcoholics. The 1982 researchers observed in applying the ratio of adults to children that the Booz-Allen study made a mathematical error. The estimate with this "error" was 1.2 million COAs in Pennsylvania.

4   The researchers utilized the 10 million estimate provided by "Facts on Alcoholism and the Family" of the New York City National Council on Alcoholism. The researchers report that there had been a very crude estimate given earlier by NIAAA of approximately 9 million.

5   Marcia Russell, Cynthia Henderson and Sheila B. Blume, Children of Alcoholics: A Review of the Literature, Children of Alcoholics Foundation, 1985.

6   W. B. Clark and L. Midanik, "Alcohol Use and Alcohol Problems Among U. S. Adults: Results of the 1979 National Survey," Monograph No. 1: Alcohol Consumption and Related Problems, DHHS Publication No. (ADM) 82-1190, 1982.

7   See Children of Alcoholics Foundation, Inc., Children of Alcoholics in the Medical System: Hidden Problems, Hidden Costs, 1990, and Migs Woodside, Children of Alcoholics: A Report to Hugh L. Carey, Governor, State of New York, New York State Division of Alcoholism and Alcohol Abuse, 1982.

8   While it is common terminology for many in the alcohol field to refer to a person who may have previously had an alcohol problem but is currently in recovery as an "alcoholic," this is not the sense in which the currency of "alcoholic" is used herein. Rather, the term is used to indicate one who manifests current symptoms of alcohol dependence or alcohol abuse.

9   Michael E. Hilton, "What I Would Most Like To Know: How Many Alcoholics are there in the United States?" British Journal of Addiction 84:459-460, 1989.

10   B. S. Grant and T. C. Harford, The Relationship Between Ethanol Intake and DSM-III Alcohol Reporting, Journal of Studies on Alcohol, v. 51, #5, 1990.

11   The DSM-III-R definition of "alcohol dependency" includes "alcohol abuse." Therefore the two terms are not mutually exclusive; "alcohol abusers" are therefore a subset of those who are "alcohol dependent."

12   It could be argued that to be an "alcoholic" one would, strictly speaking, have to meet the alcohol dependency DSM-III-R criteria, but the alcohol abuse criteria alone would not qualify. This latter category would, under this argument, represent abusive drinking patterns at some stage of life, but do not necessarily amount to, or develop into, alcoholism, per se. However, the additional health risk factors to children can and are produced by a parent meeting the alcohol abuse criteria are potentially just as significant. Thus, we have used an either/or criterion of inclusion. This appears to be conceptually consistent with the attempts of the 1982 and 1985 researchers.

13   The authors are in the process of calculating the COA estimates as reported herein for the alternative definition as well, and these will be reported in a separate study.

14   B. S. Grant, et. al., "Prevalence of DSM-III-R Alcohol Abuse and Dependence: U. S., 1988," Epidemiological Bulletin #27, Alcohol Health & Research World, 15-1, (In Press). The "or" is inclusive.

15   The NIAAA data given by Table 1 are significant to the two decimal places as they are presented. However, given the differ ent methodologies of estimating parental period prevalence, number of children in different ranges and the other factors in this study, the reader should draw no implication from the number of "significant" figures provided that this methodology or our calculations have that degree of precision.

16   e.g. Migs Woodside, op. cit. and Booz-Allen and Hamilton, Incorporated, op. cit.

17   United States Census Bureau, "Total Population Estimates: 1988."

18 National Center for Health Statistics, Vital and Health Statistics: Supplement to the Monthly Vital Statistics Report: Advance Reports, 1986, Public Health Service, March 1990. The data are for 1986 whereas the prevalence and population data are for 1988. The fertility numbers are relatively stable and this disparity produces little error.

19 The sum is less than 100% in that a few children are born to fathers under age 18.

20 If the alcoholic fertility rate were greater than the non-alcoholic, then this methodology would underestimate the COA estimate. If less, there would be an overestimate. There is no definitive research that we have been able to find on this subject. There is anecdotal research evidence that young alcoholic males divorce and remarry at a rate that exceeds the non-alcoholics and also are more fertile. There is also evidence that as alcoholism progresses sterility and impotence increases and fertility thereby decreases. Since most children are fathered by relatively young men, it is possible that the behavioral pattern of the young and middle age alcoholic male increases fertility more than the physiological effects of the alcoholism diminishes it in the later stages. Generally marriage rates of alcoholics do not seem to differ than those of non-alcoholics, however divorce rates are higher. When one considers the remarriage factor and the fact that the divorce may have taken place after children have been conceived and/or born. See Thomas J. Paolino, Jr. et al., "Statistics on Alcoholic Marriages: An Overview," The International Journal of the Addictions, 13(8), 1285-1293, 1978.
Charles M. Unkovic and Gloria K. Irrgang, Double of Nothing: The Double Alcoholic Marriage, University of Central Florida, Orlando, January 1981.

21 It is possible to estimate the weighted female prevalence more precisely by following a maternal age analysis similar to the male one that has been done. This would require much more detailed analysis of the NIAAA survey unpublished data in order to match the age categories for maternal fertility. The gain in precision was considered much to small to be worth the effort.

22 In the 1988 NHIS survey, raw data that could likely produce a relatively accurate measure was obtained, but it has not yet been analyzed.

23 Charlotte A. Schoenborn, Exposure to Alcoholism in the Family: United States, 1988, National Center for Health Statistics, Advance Date Number 205, September 30, 1991
Page 17

Developmental Assessment of Children of Alcoholics

Jeannette L. Johnson, Ph.D., Jon E. Rolf, Ph.D.,
Stuart Tiegel, L.C.S.W., David McDuff, M.D.

I. Introduction

Reviews of the research conducted during the last several decades on studies of the prevalence of alcoholism in the United States, such as Russell's (1991), substantiate the belief that the children of alcoholics (COAs) are at high risk for alcoholism. A great many questions, however, remain unanswered about how to measure premorbid risk factors in the children of alcoholics and how to demonstrate their causal roles. These questions about risk assessment and function for children of alcoholics are debated by clinical, applied and basic research disciplines; depending upon the discipline, different approaches are used to answer them. All too frequently, the approaches to these questions about risk are contradictory; subsequently, so are the answers. Searles and Windle (1991) address this dilemma by stating that:

> "One reason for this [conflict between disciplines] is that good science requires experimental rigor at the expense of what sometimes appears to be ecological validity, while clinical data can be easily compromised with respect to empirical validity and reliability but retain substantial real-world meaning for specific individuals. Similarly, clinicians, and to some extent researchers, tend to ignore or reinterpret research findings that do not fit their theoretical orientation or personal world view, and researchers often dismiss clinical reports as uncontrolled or riddled with theoretical over interpretation" (page 2).

Gaining better understanding of the etiological functions of risk as well as skill in risk assessment in COAs would represent important scientific progress. Such progress, at the same time, could well enhance clinical practice by pointing to more effective prevention and early treatment methods.

An important first step towards making scientific progress in moving from speculations about risk factors to testable risk models involves coming to grips with the need for a common language of risk factors and a common understanding of available and to-be-developed assessment methods. Our answers to clinical, applied, or basic scientific questions about COAs depend upon the quality of the data obtained from our assessments. This is true whether the assessment is a paper and pencil question-naire, a laboratory performance test, a clinical interview, or a mere conversation. Progress in cataloging and understanding the assessment process can serve as an important building block for a common language with which to communicate better progress in COA risk research. Practically, if researchers understood differ-ent assessments, or at best used common assessment instru-ments in standard ways, they would be able to compare findings and discuss, with confidence, reasons for commonalities and differences.

Assessment for purposes of description or testing causal link-ages involve complicated tasks, ones that are not easily met without considerable effort. Each discipline struggles to apply sensitive and specific assessments to test their theories of risk for children of alcoholics. However, assessing any child, and especially a child who may be at risk for an assortment of traits, states, or attributes hypothesized to underlie (or mark) a developmental risk factor, is a complex undertaking. Which domain do you assess with what instrument, at what age (or stage of risk expression), and how often? These are thorny questions.

It is the primary goal of this paper to wrestle with some of these issues and to provide a framework for assessing children of alcoholics that would be useful to both researchers and service providers working with COAs. Hopefully, this paper will provide the impetus for a continuing discussion on assessment strategies so that a consensus might emerge on optimal assessment plans for children at risk for alcoholism.

A secondary goal of this paper is to present the issues related to assessment within the context of a developmental framework. Through proper assessment of the child's behavior, and within the context of understanding normal developmental attempts at mastery, we can track the developmental trajectories of both adaptive and maladaptive behaviors. Within this developmental framework, we argue that normal childhood behavior includes the child's innate drive to experience their world by attempting to master the objects, events, and people in their environment. For

COAs, we may observe that developmentally normal attempts at mastery are adaptive behaviors in a dysfunctional environment. Nevertheless, these behaviors may become the beginnings of habits which, in a different context and at a different age, might become maladaptive and which some might label 'codependent' in adulthood.

We have organized our review into three sections. We start by presenting a review of the behavioral assessments that have been done on children of alcoholics in the United States within the past three decades. The assessments of COAs across psychophysiological and biological functional domains, while important, have been reserved for another review. It is beyond the scope of this paper to address all these assessment domains. This paper, therefore, is limited to those issues relevant to the behavioral assessment of school-aged children of alcoholics. The second section critiques the current assessment procedures against the background of developmental theory and the relevance of understanding developmental methodology as part of the assessment process. The final section presents recommendations for a comprehensive assessment battery for children of alcoholics and discusses the need for new assessment techniques with these children. It is hoped that these recommendations will be the beginning of a discussion that will foster a consensus on the most appropriate assessment battery for children of alcoholics.

II. Review of the Assessments of Children of Alcoholics

In this section we review three decades of published reports on the behavioral assessment methods applied to school-aged children of alcoholics. This is not a review of the literature on the differences between children of alcoholics and children of non-alcoholics. Over 20 reviews, some quite excellent, of the literature on these differences exist (Adler & Raphael, 1983; Austin & Prendergast, 1991; Chafetz, Blane, & Hill, 1971; Corder, McRee, & Rohrer, 1984; el-Guebaly, 1986; el-Guebaly & Offord, 1977, 1979; Galanter, 1991; Johnson & Bennett, 1988; Johnson & Rolf, 1990; Johnson, Sher, & Rolf, 1992; Plant, Orford, & Grant, 1989; Russell, Henderson, & Blume, 1985; Searles & Windle, 1991; Sher, 1991; Thalinger & Kovanek, 1988; von Knorring, 1991; Warner & Rosett, 1975; Watters & Theimer, 1978; West & Prinz, 1987; Wilson & Orford, 1978; Windle, 1989).

The following criteria were used for inclusion in the review of behavioral assessments of school-aged children of alcoholics:

Sample Definition:

1. Studies of COAs were included if their parents had a primary diagnosis of alcoholism; parents with secondary diagnoses of alcoholism were not included.

2. School-aged children of alcoholics are defined as those between the ages of 5 and 18. Studies of infants, pre-schoolers, or college-aged youth are not included.

3. Studies reviewed were those published samples of children from the United States. This review strategy was used to alleviate problems associated with the translation of English tests into foreign language equivalents. However, some excellent studies from other countries are available, i.e., Scandinavia (Aronson et al. 1985; Cloninger, Sigvaardsson, & Bohman, 1988; Knop et al. 1985; Nylander & Rydelius, 1982; Rydelius, 1981; Zetterstrom & Nylander, 1985), Portugal (de Mendonca et al. 1985), France (Lemoine et al. 1968), Russia (Shurygin, 1974), Puerto Rico (Rubio-Stipec et al. 1991), Yugoslavia (Miketic, 1972), Canada (el-Guebaly et al. 1978), Germany (Steinhausen, Nestler, & Huth, 1982), Great Britain (Bell & Cohen, 1981), Australia (Callan & Jackson, 1986), and Czechoslovakia (Matejcek, 1981).

4. The sampling source (i.e., parental alcoholism, childhood treatment status) was overlooked. Thus, some of the samples of children of alcoholics are of children whose alcoholic parents are in treatment, some children of alcoholics are in treatment themselves, and some children of alcoholics are also juvenile delinquents.

5. Composition of the COA sample is presented with regard to size, sex, and age. Since this is a review of assessment procedures and not group differences, control group composition is not described.

Extent of Assessments:

6. Only studies utilizing a battery of tests assessing behavior were included. Behavioral assessment was not limited to performance, but also included self-reports and informant reports of behavior. This review does not include neurophysiological or biological assessments.

Consequently, studies using primarily neuropsychological assessment techniques were not included; however, the studies that included behavioral assessment along with a neuropsychological battery were reviewed.

Table 1 presents the results of the review of 36 studies which met these six inclusion criteria. They are listed in the chronological order of their appearance in the scientific literature. These studies were gathered by two means: (1) through computerized literature searches accessing several psychological databases, and (2) with 'hands on' literature searches in journals that were not included in the computerized databases. We acknowledge that this review may be incomplete because it excludes those studies that have not been published in the scientific literature.

Our review reveals that since behavioral assessment began on children of alcoholics in the early 1960's, over 2000 children of alcoholics have been tested in the United States when you combine the samples of published studies. It is difficult to derive a precise count of the COAs who have been sampled because some of the published studies probably used the same sample of children in more than one publication.

We found a wide variety of behavioral assessments in the COA literature used over the past three decades. Although the earliest behavioral assessments of COAs were usually developed by the authors of those early studies, attempts have been made across time to use standardized assessments with normed reference groups. Table 2 lists over 70 different behavioral measures which were used to assess children of alcoholics (derived by taking a frequency count of those assessments listed in Table 1). Eighty percent of these measures were used only once and only in one particular study. The most frequently used tests (at least three or more times) are the Wide Range Achievement Test (reading, spelling, arithmetic), WISC-R/WAIS-R (verbal, performance, and full scale IQ), Child Behavior Checklist (parental reports of behavior problems; includes externalizing and internalizing syndromes), Children of Alcoholics Screening Test (children's report of concerns about their parent's drinking), Connors Teacher Rating Scale (teacher ratings of behavior problems), Family Environment Scale (parent reports of family functioning variables, such as family cohesion), Hopkins Symptom Checklist (behavioral

Table 1: Testing Children of Alcoholics: A Review of Childhood Behavioral Assessments in Chronological Order of Appearance in the Literature

Reference	Sample	Assessments
Aronson & Gilbert, 1963	41 male COAs; Age range=7 to completion of grammar school.	Personality Questionaire developed by authors (T).
Haberman, 1966	142 COAs	Childhood Symptom Checklist developed by author(P).
Cork, 1969	115 male(59) and female(56) COAs; Age range=10 to 16, mean=15.	Child Interview developed by author (C).
Kammeier, 1971	65 male(2) and female(45) COAs; Mean age=15.4(1.2).	Minnesota Counseling Inventory(C); Personal Orientation Inventory(C); Iowa Tests of Educational Development(C); Lorge-Thorndike Intelligence Tests(C).
Chafetz, Blane, & Hill, 1971	100 male(60) and female(40) COAs; Age range=2 to 19, mean=11.6.	Hospital chart review (demographics, illness, accident, school problems, and problems with the law).
Fine, Yudin, Holmes, Heinemann, 1976	39 male(21) and female(18) COAs; Age range=8 to 18, mean=12.1	Devereux Child or Adolescent Behavior Rating Scale(P); Symptom Rating Scale(P); Examination of school records(E).
Herjanic, Herjanic, Penick, Tomelleri, 1977	82 COAs; Age range=6 to 17.	Herjanic Diagnostic Interview for Children(C); PPVT(C); WRAT(C); Other psychological tests not described; Developmental Questionnaire(P); School reports(T).

Author/Year	Sample	Measures
Hughes, 1977	50 COAs (25 from Alateen); Age range=12 to 19; mean=15.44.	Profile of Mood States(C); Rosenberg Self-Esteem Scale(C); Self report of problems with the law or school(C).
Miller & Jang, 1977	147 male and female COAs.	Interviews for parents and children developed by authors.
Prewett, Spence, & Chaknis, 1981	15 male(8) and female(7) COAs; Age range=7 to 12.	Nowicki-Strickland Locus of Control (C).
Kern, Hassett, Collipp, Bridges, Solomon, & Condren 1981	20 male(10) and female(10) COAs; Age range=8 to 13.	Otis-Lennon Mental Abilities Test (C); Nowicki-Strickland Locus of Control (C).
Moos & Billings, 1982	50 male(25) and female(25) COAs from recovering parents (Mean age=14(5.7)); 23 male(11) and female(12) COAs from relapsed parents; (Mean age=10.8(6)).	Health and Daily Living Form(P); Family Environment Scale(P); Child Functioning questionnaire (P).
Ervin, Little, Streissguth, & Beck, 1984	50 male(25) and female(25) COAs; Age range=infancy to over 15 years; 66% of sample between 3 and 14 years of age.	Bayley Scales of Infant Development(C); Stanford Binet(C); WISC-R or WAIS(C); WRAT(C).
Tarter, Hegedus, Goldstein, Shelly, & Altterman, 1984	16 male COAs; Mean age=16(1.2).	WISC-R(C); PINTS(C); Detroit Tests of Learning Aptitude(C); PIAT(C); Matching Familiar Figures Test(C); MBD Checklist(C); MMPI(C).
Hegedus, Alterman, & Tarter, 1984	16 male COAs; Mean age=16(1.2).	PIAT(C); PINTS(C); MMPI(C); Family Environment Scale(C); Devereux Adolescent Behavior Scale(P).

Reference	Sample	Measures
Tarter, Hegedus, & Gavaler, 1985	16 male COAs; Mean age=16.	Childhood History MBD Checklist(C).
Jacob & Leonard, 1986	100 male(56) and female(44) COAs; Age range=10 to 18.	CBCL(P); Conners Teacher Rating Scale(T); Myklebust Pupil Rating Scale(T).
Manning, Balson, & Xenakis, 1986	Study 1: 46 male(26) and female(20) COAs; Age range=5 to 17.	Matthews Youth Test for Health(P); Jenkins Activity Survey(P).
	Study 2: 95 COAs; Age range=5 to 17, Mean age=9.9.	same as above
Marcus, 1986	40 male(15) and female(25) COAs; Age range 7 to 12.9.	PIAT(C).
Werner, 1986	49 male(22) and female(27) COAs tested longitudinally from birth to age 18.	At 10 years of age: Primary Mental Abilities Test (C); Bender-Gestalt(C).

At grade 12: California Psychological Inventory(C); Nowicki-Strickland Locus of Control (C); needs assessments done by clinical team; Standardized tests available from school. |
| Rhodes & Blackham, 1987 | 32 male(11) and female(21) COAs; Mean age=16.6. | CAST(C); demographic information; Children of Alcoholics Family Role Instrument. |
| Earls, Reich, Jung, & Cloninger, 1988 | 38 male(22) and female(16) children of 1 alcoholic parent(Mean age=11.1); 12 male(7) and female(5) children of 2 alcoholic parents(Mean age=13.9); Age range=6 to 17. | Home Environment Interview for Children(P,C); Diagnostic Interview for Children and Adolescents(P,C); Coopersmith Self-Esteem Inventory(C); Dimensions of Temperament Survey(C);Peabody Picture Vocabulary Test(C); Wide Range Achievement Test(C); Behavior Screening Questionnaire(P). |

Bennett, Wolin, & Reiss, 1988	64 male and female COAs; Age range=6 to 18, mean age=12.08(3.4).	WISC-R or WAIS-R(C); Piers-Harris Children's Self Concept Scale(C); Herjanic Diagnostic Interview for Children and Adolescents (C); CBCL(P); Conners Parent Symptom Rating Scale(P).
Roosa, Sandler, Gehring, Beals, & Cappo, 1988	Study 1: 10 male and female COAs; grades 9-12	CAST(C); Children of Alcoholic Life-Events Schedule(C).
	Study 2: 56 male(16) and female(40) COAs; Age range=14 to 18.	CAST(C); Children of Alcoholic Life-Events Schedule(C); Hopkins Symptom Checklist(C); demographic questions and other measures not reported.
Johnson & Rolf, 1988	50 male(26) and female(24) COAs; Age range=6-18, mean age=13(8.6).	WRAT(C); WISC-R or WAIS-R(C); Perceived Competence for Children(C); Project Competence Child Interview(C); CBCL(P); Conners Parents Symptom Rating Questionnaire(P); Perceived Competence for Children(P).
Drake & Vaillant, 1988	174 male COAs; Mean age=14(2).	Wechsler-Bellevue IQ(C); Emotional problem scale; Boyhood Competence Scale; Physical Health Scale; Feelings of Inadequacy Ratings(P,T, or CI); School behavior problems and truancy (T).
Roosa, Sandler, Beals, & Short, 1988	Study 1: 38 male and female COAs; Age range=14 to 19.	Depression and anxiety subscales of the Hopkins Symptom Checklist(C); Rosenberg Self-Esteem Scale(C); Adolescent Alcohol Involvement Scale(C).
	Study 2: 32 male and female COAs; Age range=14 to 18.	same as above

Rolf, Johnson, Israel, Baldwin, & Chandra, 1988	50 male(26) and female(24) COAs; Age range=6-18, mean age=13(8.6).	Center for Epidemiological Studies Depression Scale(P); CBCL(P); Childrens Depression Inventory(C); Beck Depression Inventory(C); Youth Self Report(C).
Johnson, Leonard, & Jacob, 1989	33 male and female COAs; Age range= 10 to 18, mean age=14.3(2).	Questionnaire on drinking experience and drinking style(C); Williams Temperance and Intemperance Scales(C); Reasons for Drinking Scale(C); Questionnaire on what child would do to obtain alcohol and drug use(C).
Pandina and Johnson, 1989	Time 1: 276 male(128) and female(148) COAs; Age range=12 to 18. Time 2: 270 male(124) and female(146) COAs; Age range=15 to 21 (same subjects as Time 1 but older).	Self-report questionnaires designed by the Rutgers Health and Human Development Project (use of drugs index, age of onset, frequency of use, reasons for use, conse quences of use)(C).
Tarter, Jacob, & Bremer, 1989	33 male COAs; Mean age=12.12(2.33).	Detroit Tests of Learning Aptitude(C) (plus 13 neuropsychological tests).
Tarter, Kabene, Escallier, Laird, Jacob, 1990	37 male COAs; Mean age=15.	Dimensions of Temperament Scale(C); Family Environment Scale(P).
Roosa, Beals, Sandler, & Pillow, 1990	43 male(13) and female(30) COAs; Mean age=15.6.	Hopkins Symptom Checklist(C); CAST(C); Children of Alcoholics Life Events Schedule(C); General Life Events Schedule for Children(C).
Ballard & Cummings, 1991	13 male(5) and female(8) COAs; Age range=6 to 10, mean age=7.6(1.3).	CBCL(P); Straus Conflict Tactics Scale(P); Children viewed videotapes of angry and positive adult interactions and then interviewed

		regarding their feelings and perceptions about the videotape.
Whipple & Noble, 1991	18 male COAs; Age range=10 to 15, mean age=12.3.	Personality Inventory for Children(P); High School Personality Questionnaire(C); Junior Eysenck Personality Inventory(C): Tridimensional Personality Questionnaire(C).
Stern, Kendall, & Eberhard, 1991	16 COAs, grades 1 to 5 (from special and regular education classes).	CAST(C); Friel Co-Dependency Assessment(taken by parent about themselves).

Sample Notes: Mean age=years(SD)

Test Abbreviations: CBCL=Child Behavior Checklist; CAST=Children of Alcoholics Screening Test; PIAT=Peabody Individual Achievement Test; PPVT=Peabody Picture Vocabulary Test; WRAT=Wide Range Achievement Test; PINTS=Pittsburgh Neuropsychological Test System.

Test informants: C=Child; P=Parent; T=Teacher; E=Experimenter Rating; CI=Clinician symptomatology), Peabody Individual Achievement Test, and the Rosenberg Self-Esteem Scales.

We recognize that clinicians and researchers choose assessments for different reasons, but with such a wide variety of tests used, it makes comparisons between even more studies difficult, if not impossible. Clearly there is a great need to use instruments to help between-study comparisons and to aid our understanding of the implication of the findings for further research and intervention services.

After reviewing the variety of measures used to test COAs, it appears that while some of these assessments may be necessary, they are not sufficient. The importance of understanding developmental processes in COAs and the child's active role in this process cannot be underestimated. It is possible that some COAs may experience a subtle, yet important, divergence from normal developmental pathways that has yet to be measured with existing assessment techniques. Against the background of a developmental framework, we contend below that existing assessment strategies have not adequately explored the predictive aspects of the developmental process in COAs.

II. Exploring a Developmental Framework for Assessing COA's Codependency

Developmental research shows that children of different ages think, feel, and act according to differences in cognitive and affective stages of development (Cowen, 1978; Flavell, 1977; Nannis, 1988; Piaget, 1955, 1963). Measuring these processes requires an assessment procedure that attends to normal individual differences in behavior during development; however, as the previous review demonstrated, this has rarely been done in studies of COAs. In Table 1, examination of the subject age ranges within studies shows little attention to normal developmental differences in the research design. Frequently, a single assessment instrument was used for mixed age and stage groups of subjects and, typically, only overall group mean scores and between-group mean differences were reported. Describing children

Table 2: Assessments used on Children of Alcoholics 1963-1991

Adolescent Alcohol Involvement Scale-2
Bayley Scales of Infant Development-1
Beck Depression Inventory-1
Behavior Screening Questionnaire-1
Bender-Gestalt-1
Boyhood Competence Scale-1
California Psychological Inventory-1
Center for Epidemiology Studies-Depression-1
Chart Review-1
Child Functioning Questionnaire-1
Child Behavior Checklist (CBCL)-3
Childhood History MBD Checklist-2
Childhood Symptom Checklist-1
Children of Alcoholic Screening Test-4
Children of Alcoholics Family Role Instrument-1
Children of Alcoholic Life-Events Schedule-2
Children's Depression Inventory-1
Connors Teacher Rating Scale-3
Coopersmith Self-Esteem Inventory-1
Detroit Tests of Learning Aptitude-2
Developmental Questionnaire-1
Devereux Child/Adolescent Behavior Rating Scale-2
Diagnostic Interview for Children/Adolescents-1
Dimensions of Temperament Survey-2
Drinking Experience/Style Questionnaire-1
Emotional Problem Scale-1
Family Environment Scale-3
Feelings of Inadequacy Ratings-1
General Life Events Schedule for Children-1
Health and Daily Living Form-1
Herjanic Diagnostic Interview for Children/Adolescents-2

Law problems, self report-1
Lorge-Thorndike Intelligence Tests-1
Matching Familiar Figures Tests-1
Matthews Youth Test for Health-2
Minnesota Multiphasic Personality Inventory-2
Minnesota Counseling Inventory-1
Myklebust Pupil Rating Scale-1
Needs Assessment-1
Nowicki-Strickland Locus of Control-3
Otis-Lennon Mental Abilities Test-1
Peabody Picture Vocabulary Test(PPVT)-2
Peabody Individual Achievement Test(PIAT)-4
Perceived Competence for Children-2
Personal Orientation Inventory-1
Personality Inventory for Children-1
Personality Questionnaire-1
Physical Health Scale-1
Piers-Harris Children's Self Concept Scale-1
Pittsburgh Initial Neuropsychology Test System-2
Primary Mental Abilities Test-1
Profile of Mood States-1
Project Competence Interview-1
Reasons for Drinking Scale-1
Rosenberg Self-Esteem Scales-3
Rutgers Health and Human Development Questionnaire-1
School records or problems-5
Stanford Binet-1
Strauss Conflict Tactics Scale-1
Tridimensional Personality Questionnaire-1
Videotapes of Angry and Positive Interactions-1
Wechsler-Bellevue IQ-1

High School Personality Questionnaire-1
Home Environment Interview for Children-1
Hopkins Symptom Checklist-4
Interviews developed by author for the study-2
Iowa Tests of Educational Development-1
Jenkins Activity Survey-2
Junior Eysenck Personality Inventory-1

What child would do to use AOD questionnaire-1
Wide Range Achievement Test-4
Williams Temperance and Intemperance Scales-1
WISCR or WAISR-4
Youth Self Report-1

This is a list of assessment instruments used on CoAs which were derived from the studies in Table 1. The numbers after the instrument indicate how many studies reported using it in their study.

in this manner conflicts with acceptable standards for testing developmental processes and differences between groups of children.

Many behavioral scientists and laypersons are familiar with Piaget's explanatory model of cognitive development during childhood (Piaget, 1951, 1955, 1963, 1970). We can outline his model here and speculate how the cognitive processes of children developing in families headed by alcoholics might develop into codependency. Further, we can speculate how such adaptations are both normal (i.e., common) and predictable products of typical cognitive processes.

A Cognitive Developmental Framework

Piaget describes how the different ways of knowing and acting on the environment (e.g., cognitive development) change in a systematic fashion as children grow older. In his model, cognitive development is viewed as a natural progressive process, one motivated by the child's innate tendency to organize experiences and adapt to predictable environmental events according to the typical cognitive structures of each developmental stage. As described by Piaget, cognitive developmental stages occur in a hierarchical sequence: sensorimotor, preoperations, concrete operations, and formal operations.

While most people remember best Piaget's (1963) sequence of stages, he described the **process** of cognitive change that influences the ways children come to know about themselves and their world. To Piaget it is the mechanism of change, the movement from and through each stage, that is crucial to understanding the developmental course. Measuring this progress across and through stages is difficult and while it may be convenient to divide development into stages, development is a continuum that may not be linear, but instead consist of minor oscillations. These minor oscillations propel the course of cognitive progress, which proceeds by self-regulation, coordination, and equilibrium (Flavell, 1963). Equilibrium refers to the tendency for children to adapt to events, people, and objects in the environment to create a balance between oneself and the environment. When a child experiences an unfamiliar or unpredicted event, the motivation for regaining equilibrium propels change as the child experiences a 'beneficial perturbation' (Flavell, 1977), or disequilibrium. For example, a child can experience disequilibrium when his/her alcoholic parent behaves in a deviant way. Disequilibrium produces a state of cognitive conflict, which the child resolves by cognitively restructuring reality: parents are people who get mad, scare their own children, or fall down and go to sleep.

Adapting to the objects, events, and people in the environment through cognitive organization and reorganization occurs with two complementary processes: assimilation and accommodation. Assimilation and accommodation happen simultaneously and often without the conscious awareness of the individual. When children assimilate something, they adapt the external stimuli to their own existing cognitive structures (or patterns of reality); when they accommodate, they adapt their cognitive structures (i.e., reality) to include the new stimuli. Thus, through assimila-tion, the events, people, or objects in the environment are inter-preted according to the ways one already thinks about things (Flavell, 1977). For example, when children first encounter objects or events never before experienced, they will try to change them into something they have already experienced and are familiar with, regardless of the properties of the object. For example, an alcoholic parent who has drunk him or herself into unconscious-ness is thought to be asleep due to fatigue. In this way, the child acts on the object or event in a manner that is already familiar to their repertoire.

In the process of accommodation, however, existing cognitive structures must be adjusted to new experiences that don't 'fit in'. In the case of the child experiencing a new object, event, or person, their behavioral repertoire is adjusted; if the adult reacts unexpectedly due to the child's actions (e.g., a drunk parent who slaps a child who approaches seeking attention), the child learns about new properties of this person and adjusts his or her behav-ioral repertoire to include new ways of acting (e.g., when a parent has been drinking alcohol and looks or talks in a different way, the child learns to avoid the parent).

In summary, assimilation and accommodation, occurring simul-taneously in order to establish equilibrium in the face of cognitive conflict (disequilibrium), happen with each familiar and unfamiliar experience of an object, event, or person. Disequilibrium, or cognitive conflict, produces a state of cognitive tension which the child is driven to resolve through further cognitive exploration. Each time a child confronts an experience, the way in which they understand the event is, in part, shaped by their current cognitive structures. That is, they bend (or even distort) reality so as to make it fit within current modes of cognitive organization. Healthy children, including COAs, can even come to create a reality that cannot be shared or understood by children who have a different experiential history. In this way a balance is maintained in their representation of the world. However, as objects, events, or people are physically or mentally manipulated, current modes of cognitive organization are also modified by the experience. Hence, although we alter reality to fit with our present cognitive structures, our cognitive structures can be altered slightly to fit with new aspects of the world.

Constructivism in COAs

In Piaget's model, development is seen as a self-generated cycle. Children therefore are not seen as passive recipients of information, but rather actively construct or build their conception of the world through both physical and mental manipulations. The child, while constructing reality, is not passively absorbing an adult's conceptualization of reality nor passively replicating it, but actually constructing it according to his or her own interpretation and particular stage of cognitive development. Depending upon the stage of development and the sequence of experiences, children's concepts of things vary according to the characteristics of that stage. Different stages of cognitive development are characterized by some types of thinking that often appear illogical, inaccurate, and fanciful; yet this type of thinking is quite normal (i.e., Piaget, 1951). For example, a preschooler may interpret a drunk parent's talking to an unseen person as the same kind of imaginary friend that preschoolers like to play with.

The imagination and fanciful thinking of childhood serves many purposes. In general, though, imagination (or fanciful thinking) is one way children mentally explore the attributes of potential events without actually acting them out. Such cognitive exploration can serve as an expression of cognitive mastery, the feeling of accomplishment derived from engaging in and mastering difficult problem solving tasks. The importance of this activity has been repeatedly emphasized in the literature (Asarnow, Carlson & Guthrie, 1987; Freedman et al. 1978). The ability to problem solve is also considered to be an essential part of resilience; it is the ability to recover effective functioning after experiencing negative consequences of living (Rolf et al., 1990). Werner (1986) describes resilient children as those children who actively solve problems in the face of considerable adversity. Werner (1984) also suggests that one of the four central characteristics of resiliency is an active, evocative approach toward solving life's problems which enables the child to successfully understand and reinterpret emotionally hazardous experiences during development.

Active problem solving is expressed differently at different ages and its measurement would require different tools across stages. Six to 12 year old children think things out concretely; they'll try to work out complex problems with specific examples and not hypothetical constructs symbolic of a generalized category of a problem. For example, when COAs in the stage of concrete operations want to solve the problems of their alcoholic parents, they will do so concretely. They pour the wine out of the bottle so there is none to drink; they may clean the house or cook the food when the parents neglect caretaking duties. These COAs become problem solvers through physical activities. In the stage of formal operations (12 years and older), however, COAs are able to hypothesize about the problems resulting from parental behaviors and therefore are able to mentally manipulate a range of possible causes and solutions for the problems; they are not tied to the here and now of concrete solutions. COAs in this stage may try to listen to the parents' interpretations of their problems and suggest numerous 'what if' problem solving solutions. Their minds become a workshop of problem solving strategies (Siegler & Jenkins, 1989).

Active problem solving is one of the most important self-regulated protective processes available to a child in a truly dysfunctional household. Active problem solving helps the child in his/her attempts to cope with adversity. When problem solving is successful, it resolves cognitive conflict, which, in turn, establishes internal equilibrium, if only for a little while. The generalization of a successful problem solving strategy learned during childhood in an alcoholic household to other situations may prove maladaptive or dysfunctional. Not all problem solving strategies that COAs learn will be appropriate to generalize to non-alcoholic environments. Compensating for an alcoholic parent's behavior may have been necessary for a young COA to grow up, but continuing this behavior into adulthood may prove problematic. For example, an adult COA who compensates for a new companion's problematic behaviors may reinforce 'codependency' and prevent further development of competence in both individuals.

The point being made is that cognitive activity, and hence, problem solving, is necessary for the resolution of cognitive conflict. The **absence** of problem solving activity in childhood may be a risk factor for future depression. All children need to discover which strategies work effectively, which don't, and where newly discovered strategies are appropriate and inappropriate (Siegler & Jenkins, 1989). The structure of cognitive activity for children of alcoholics and non-alcoholics is the same; the challenge is to discover the appropriate assessment methods that demonstrate that it is the functionality of the problem solving strategy that is different.

III. Applying a Developmental Framework to the Assessment of COAs

This review of the literature suggests that the assessments used on COAs, to date, have been somewhat deficient in their relevance to developmental processes associated with hypothesized risk factors for future psychopathology and substance abuse. The good news, however, is that the assessment process has recently become more scientifically systematic and less anecdotal. This is partially a result of evolving progress in the assessment field, and partially a result of examining the available information on COAs and recognizing the complexity of etiological processes. The next steps in deciding on adequate assessment strategies for COAs will most likely consider complex issues related to the embeddedness of problem behaviors in different contexts at different ages.

How to do it: Caveats

Zucker and Fitzgerald (1991) suggest that adopting a developmental methodology will help us understand adaptive functioning in COAs, how early maladaptive behaviors are created, and the contexts in which they appear, linger, and diminish. However, how does one adequately and operationally define a source of risk for a COA given the possibility of the existence of multiple genetic processes and environmental changes that may interact at any point? We list five consequences of adopting a developmental framework for assessing COAs:

1. **Individual Differences** Through the individual and systematic assessment of COAs, individual patterns, styles, or strategies of cognitive organization may be identified that differentiate COAs from children of non-alcoholics within or across developmental stages. Thus, measuring the individual child's adaptability or adaptation to objects, events, and people, and not necessarily with norms and group averages, is necessary.

2. **Attention to Developmental Assessment** Children who come from dysfunctional homes may respond differently to problem solving tasks, interview questions, and people, depending upon where the assessment is performed or the perceived threat of the alcoholic parent's interpretation of the elicited response. Developmental change precludes simple and unitary assessment procedures in children of different stages and ages; a particular test appropriate at one age is not necessarily appropriate at another. Younger children do not understand tests using abstract symbolic concepts. Similarly, younger children must be asked questions with simpler language. Furthermore, assessments purporting to measure the feelings and behaviors through the child's verbal responses are not always sufficiently representative of the target phenomena that may occur in their natural environment.

3. **Continuity and Discontinuity** It may be necessary to evaluate the dynamic process of developmental continuity and discontinuities of the target behavior being assessed. How many assessment occasions are adequate to measure stability and instability of behaviors across time or circumstance? Assessing behavior many times would also allow us to look at the turning points of certain behaviors and answer the question of whether or not critical periods exist.

4. **Interacting Risk Factors** Converging evidence about social, behavioral, and health problems has suggested that many negative behavioral outcomes are interrelated (Donovan & Jessor, 1985; Hundleby, 1987; Jessor & Jessor, 1977). Be cautious in believing that the chosen sub-set of promising variables selected for measurement will be sufficient to test an etiological model adequately. Much depends

upon knowledge of previously significant findings, our own training and biases, and the theoretically based hypotheses influencing the research procedures (Johnson & Rolf, 1990). Since adaptation involves complex processes resulting from the interplay of personal and environmental factors, a good assessment would include the assessment of many domains of behavior over time.

5. **Resilience** Many clinicians and researchers are seeking to understand the meaning of resilience, especially in the lives of children of alcoholics (Cowen et al. 1991; Cowen & Work, 1988; Garmezy & Tellegen, 1984; Rolf et al. 1990; Werner, 1989; Werner & Smith, 1982). With the exception of work of Emmy Werner, measurement of resilience in COAs has been overlooked. The writings of Garmezy and Werner provide useful clues to assessment.

What to Assess?

Zucker and Fitzgerald (1991) suggest that the literature has shown six separate areas that indicate causal links of risk for alcoholism among adolescent children of alcoholics. Perhaps it is to these areas we should first look:

1. Antisocial behavior or aggressive activity;

2. Difficulty in achievement-related activity, such as poorer school performance or less productivity in high school;

3. Diminished or deficient affiliative behaviors. For example, males who later become alcoholic are more loosely connected to others. The data has shown interpersonal deficits (less dependent, less considerate, less accepting of dependency), greater likelihood of leaving home early, and being more indifferent to mothers and siblings as a teenager;

4. Presence of increased marital conflict in the parental home;

5. Dysfunctional parent-child interaction (e.g., inadequate or lax parental supervision, lack of parental interest or affection for child, or inadequate contact) and

6. Inadequate role models.

In addition to measuring degree of risk, we also need to examine the emergence and development of protective processes and problem solving strategies that COAs use in the face of adversity.

Cowen and his colleagues (1991) suggest that a triad of protective factors is associated with stress resilient children that include: (1) the child's positive temperament and disposition; (2) a close, warm family relationship; (3) extrafamilial support (e.g., teachers, clergy). Perhaps, again, it is to these three areas we should look to examine the potential protective factors among COAs.

What to Use?

On a more technical level, assessment of children of alcoholics requires a thoughtful selection from available assessment tools. Achenbach and McConaughy (1987) recommend the following psychometric principles to aid in measurement decisions: (1) employ standardized procedures; (2) use multiple, aggregate items to sample each targeted aspect of functioning; (3) use measures permitting normative age appropriate reference groups; and (4) use psychometrically sound measure which have demonstrated reliability and validity within the targeted subject's developmental stage and specific age group. To these we add:

(1) Follow the principles set forth in the <u>Standards for Educational and Psychological Testing</u> (APA, 1986);

(2) Leave test construction to those who know how to implement proper psychometric procedures. Even though new measures and assessments for children appear with regularity in the literature (Cowen et al. 1991; Rohrbeck, Azar, & Wagner, 1991; Silverman et al. 1991), it is best to wait for reports on validity and reliability before using them.

(3) Use trained personnel to perform the assessment. As Johnson and Rolf (1990) suggest, interpersonal interactions with the COA could confound the results of any test. In a good testing session, it is the child's response to the task at hand, and not their response to the ability of the experimenter, that is desired.

(4) Listen without prejudice. In an area that attends so closely to what the child and the parent has to say, it is important to listen without giving away answers; thus, when interviewing children, probe their thinking without making their verbal reports something you want or expect to hear.

Broadband Screening Tools

The National Institute on Drug Abuse has developed the Adolescent Assessment/Referral System (AARS) (NIDA, 1987), an assessment tool limited to youth aged 12 to 19 (see Tarter, 1990 for a complete description). The first phase consists of a problem screening tool, the Problem Oriented Screening Instrument for Teenagers (POSIT), a 139 item screen designed to identify problems in need of further assessment in ten functional areas (substance use, behavior patterns, health status, psychiatric disorder, social skills, family system, school adjustment, work, peer relationships, and leisure/recreation). It is a good screen, but the POSIT itself does not provide comprehensive assessment; instead, it will indicate if further, in-depth assessment is required in any of the ten functional areas.

Comprehensive Assessment Battery

The AARS has compiled a Comprehensive Assessment Battery, a battery of instruments for each of the ten areas selected on the basis of recommendations of national experts in adolescent assessment and treatment. Table 3 presents the CAB recommended assessment tools for each of the ten functional areas addressed by the AARS. The AARS manual provides descriptions of the instruments, along with information on how to obtain them, administration time, and cost.

The Need for Alternative Approaches to Creating an Assessment Package for COAs

Findings from published research have generally pointed to the insufficiency of single cause explanatory accounts of problem behaviors in children (Searles and Windle, 1991). Multifactorial models appear more relevant but require more and better measurement of their constructs. Other than the tests recommended in the AARS, several others are specific to the problems of COAs and also fulfill the criteria of Achenbach and McGonaughy (1987). Using their developmental framework for assessment, five axes are proposed in Table 4, Appendix A: parent reports, teacher reports, cognitive assessment, physical assessment, and direct assessment of the child. For COAs, we add a sixth axis, the assessment of processes contributing to resiliency. In Appendix A

Table 3: Comprehensive Assessment Battery Tools from the AARS

Functional Area	Specific Measures
Substance Use/Abuse	Personal Experience Inventory Adolescent Diagnostic Interview
Physical Health Status	Physical examination and lab work Physician Report Form
Mental Health Status	Diagnostic Interview Schedule for Children Brief Symptom Inventory
Family Relationships	Family Assessment Measure Parent-Adolescent Relationship Questionnaire
Peer Relations	Piers Harris Self-Concept Scale Behavior Problem Checklist
Educational Status	WAIS-R, WISC-R Woodcock-Johnson Psychoeducational Test Battery
Vocational Status	Career Maturity Inventory Generalizable Skills Curriculum
Social Skills	Social Skills Rating System Matson Evaluation of Social Skills with Youngsters
Leisure and Recreation	Social Adjustment Inventory for Children and Adolescents Leisure Diagnostic Battery Physical Activity Assessment
Aggressive Behavior/ Delinquency	Youth Self-Report National Youth Survey Delinquency Scale

Table 4: Multiaxial Assessment

Age Range	Axis 1 Parent Reports	Axis 2 Teacher Reports	Axis 3 Cognitive Assessment	Axis 4 Physical Assessment	Axis 5 Direct Observation	Axis 6 Resilience
6 to 11	CBCL Dev. Hx. DICA HEIC LEQ-P	TRF School Records PIAT	WISC-III WRAT-R (Level 1)	Modified Physician-Report Form	Jr. Eysenck LEQ-C Perceived Comp. YSR (11 year olds) CDI (8 to 15) STAIC DICA Alcohol/Drug Hx.	HEIC
12 to 18	CBCL Dev. Hx DICA HEIC LEQ-P	TRF School Records	WISC-III (to 16) WAIS-R (after 16) WRAT-R (Level 2) PIAT	Physician-Report Form	HSPQ LEQ-A (14 to 19) Perceived Comp. YSR (11 to 18) BDI (after 16) STAIC DICA PEI	HEIC

we present some measures for consideration for these six axes relevant to the latter two stages of cognitive development: concrete operations (6 to 12 year-olds) and formal operations (12 year-olds and older). We also recognize that defining any assessment battery is a considerable task requiring consideration of many viewpoints; we present this as a preliminary framework for starting purposes only.

What is needed are consensus building workshops with COA researchers, clinicians, and expert advisors to outline the ideal assessment battery for COAs. Understanding the COA's construction of reality, the process of change, problem solving strategies used in the resolution of cognitive conflict, and the child's adaptation to a dysfunctional household will need to be explored with developmental techniques. The laboratory assessment process ignores the contextual embeddedness of the child's responses (Zucker and Fitzgerald, 1991). Contextual embeddedness, referring to the interweaving of context and child, is an important variable in understanding how and where the COA's behavior is stable or unstable. This is especially important in trying to understand the behavior of children who might change the way they behave according to the context of their response; more specifically, COAs may change their responses according to the context of the alcoholic parents' behavior or expectation in order to avoid trauma or abuse. We believe that a novel assessment for COAs is necessary that will integrate the clinician's understanding of the COA's behavior according to the context of the alcoholic home and the researcher's need for proper psychometrics.

References

Achenbach, T.M. (1978). The Child Behavior Profile, I: boys aged 6-11. Journal of Consulting and Clinical Psychology, 46, 478-488.

Achenbach, T.M., & Edelbrock, C.S. (1979). The Child Behavior Profile II: boys aged 12-16 and girls aged 6-11 and 12-16. Journal of Consulting and Clinical Psychology, 47, 223-233.

Achenbach, T.M, & Edelbrock, C. (1987). Manual for the Youth Self-Report and Profile. Burlington, VT: University of Vermont Department of Psychiatry.

Achenbach, T.M., & Edelbrock, C. (1986). *Manual for the Teacher's Report Form and Teacher Version of the Child Behavior Profile*. Burlington, VT: University of Vermont, Department of Psychiatry.

Achenbach, T.M. & McConaughy, S.H. (1987). *Empirically based assessment of child and adolescent psychopathology: Practical applications*. Newbury Park, CA: Sage Publications.
Adler, R., & Raphael, B. (1983). Children of alcoholics. *Australian and New Zealand Journal of Psychiatry, 17*, 3-8.

American Psychological Association. (1986). *Standards for Educational and Psychological Testing*. Washington, DC: American Psychological Association.

Aronson, H., & Gilbert, A. (1963). Preadolescent sons of male alcoholics. *Archives of General Psychiatry, 3*, 235-241.

Aronson, M., Kyllerman, M., Sabel, K.G., Sandin, B., & Olegard, R. (1985). Children of alcoholic families. *Acta Paediatrica Scandinavica, 74*, 27-35.

Asarnow, J., Carlson, g., & Guthrie, D. (1987). Coping strategies, self-perceptions,hopelessness, and perceived family environments in depressed and suicidal children. *Journal of Consulting and Clinical Psychology, 55*, 361-366.

Austin, G., & Prendergast, M. (1991). Children of substance abusers. *Prevention Research Update, 8(Winter)*, 1-67.

Ballard, M., & Cummings, E.M. (1991). Response to adults' angry behavior in children of alcoholic and nonalcoholic parents. *Journal of Genetic Psychology, 151(2)*, 195-209.

Beck, A.T. & Beamesderfer, A. (1974). Psychological measurements in psychopharmacology. In P. Pichot (ed.), *Modern problems in pharmacopsychiatry, 7*, (pp. 151-169), Paris:Karger.

Beck, A.T., & Beck, R.W. (1972). Screening depressed patients in family practice: A rapid technique. *Postgraduate Medicine, 52*, 81-85.

Bell, B., & Cohen, R. (1981). The Bristol Social Adjustment Guide: Comparison between the offspring of alcoholic and non-alcoholic mothers. *British Journal of Clinical Psychology, 20*, 93-95.

Bennett, L.A., Wolin, S.J., & Reiss, D. (1988). Cognitive, behavioral, and emotional problems among school-age children of alcoholic parents. *American Journal of Psychiatry, 145(2)*, 185-190.

Callan, V.J., & Jackson, D. (1986). Children of alcoholic fathers and recovered alcoholic fathers: Personal and family functioning. _Journal of Studies on Alcohol, 47(2),_ 180-182.

Cattell, R.B., Cattell, M.D., & Johns, E. (1984). _Manual and norms for the High School Personality Questionnaire._ Champaign, Ill: Institute for Personality and Ability Testing.

Chafetz, M.E., Blane, H.T., & Hill, M.J. (1971). Children of alcoholics: Observations in a child guidance clinic. _Quarterly Journal of Studies on Alcohol, 32,_ 687-698.

Cloninger, C.R., Sigvardsson, S., & Bohman, M. (1988). Childhood personality predicts alcohol abuse in young adults. _Alcoholism: Clinical and Experimental Research, 12(4),_ 494-505.

Corder, B.F., McRee, C., & Rohrer, H. (1984). A brief review of literature on daughters of alcoholic fathers. _North Carolina Journal of Mental Health, 10(20),_ 37-43.

Cork, R.M. (1969). _The Forgotten Children: A Study of Children with Alcoholic Parents._ Toronto, Addiction Research Foundation: Don Mills, General Publishing.

Cowen, P.A. (1978). _Piaget with Feeling: Cognitive, Social, and Emotional Dimensions._ New York: Holt, Rinehart and Winston.

Cowen, E.L., & Work, W.C. (1988). Resilient children, psychological wellness and primary prevention. _American Journal of Community Psychology, 16,_ 591-607.

Cowen, E.L., Work, W.C., Hightower, A.D., Wyman, P.A., Parker, G.R., & Lotyczewski, B.S. (1991). Toward the development of a measure of perceived self-efficacy in children. _Journal of Clinical Child Psychology, 20(2),_ 169-178.

de Mendonca, M.M., de Matos, A.P., da Costa Matta, A. (1978). Poor scholastic performance in children of alcoholic fathers. _Joral da Sociedade de Ciencias Medicas de Lisboa, 142(1-2),_ 67-96.

Drake, R.E., & Vaillant, G.E. (1988). Predicting alcoholism and personality disorder in a 33-year longitudinal study of children of alcoholics. _British Journal of Addiction, 83,_ 799-807.

Donovan, J.E., & Jessor, R. (1985). Structure of problem behavior in adolescence and young adulthood. _Journal of Consulting and Clinical Psychology, 53,_ 890-904.

Dunn, L.M. (1965). _Peabody Individual Achievement Test._ American Guidance Service, Inc.

Earls, F., Reich, W., Jung, K.G., & Cloninger, C.R. (1988). *Psychopathology in children of alcoholic an antisocial parents. Alcoholism: Clinical and Experimental Research, 12(4)*, 481-487.

el-Guebaly, N. (1986). *Risk research in affective disorders and alcoholism: Epidemiological surveys and trait markers. Canadian Journal of Psychiatry, 31*, 352-361.

el-Guebaly, N., & Offord, D.R. (1977). *The offspring of alcoholics: A critical review. American Journal of Psychiatry, 134*, 357-365.

el-Guebaly, N., & Offord, D.R. (1979). *On being the offspring of an alcoholic:An update. Alcoholism: Clinical and Experimental Research, 3(2)*, 148-157.

el-Guebaly, N., Offord, D., Sullivan, K., & Lynch, G. (1978). *Psychosocial adjustment of the offspring of psychiatric inpatients. Canadian Psychiatric Association Journal, 23*, 281-291.

Ervin, C.S., Little, R.E., Streissguth, A.P., & Beck, D.E. (1984). *Alcoholic fathering and it's relation to child's intellectual development: A pilot investigation. Alcoholism: Clinical and Experimental Research, 8(4)*, 362-365.

Eysenck, S.B.G. (1968). *Manual for the Junior Eysenck Personality Inventory. San Diego, CA: Educational and Industrial Testing Service.*

Fine, E., Yudin, L., Holmes, L., & Heinemann, S. (1976). *Behavioral disorders in children with parental alcoholism. Annals of the New York Academy of Sciences, 273*, 507-517.

Flavell, J. (1963). *The Developmental Psychology of Jean Piaget. New York: D. Van Nostrand Company, Inc.*

Flavell, J. (1977). *Cognitive Development. Englewood Cliffs, New Jersey: Prentice-Hall.*

Freedman, B., Donahoe, C., Rosenthal, L., Schlundt, D., & McFall, R. (1978). *A social-behavioral analysis of skill deficits in delinquent and nondelinquent boys. Journal of Consulting and Clinical Psychology, 46*, 1448-1462.

Galanter, M. (1991). *Recent Developments in Alcoholism, Volume 9, Children of Alcoholics. New York:Plenum Press.*

Garmezy, N. (1985). *Revision of the Life Events Questionnaire. Unpublished manuscript, University of Minnesota.*

Garmezy, N. (1987). *Scoring the Adolescent Life Events Questionnaire. Unpublished manuscript, University of Minnesota.*

Garmezy, N. & Tellegen, A. (1984). *Studies of stress-resistant children: Methods, variables and preliminary findings.* In F. Morrison, C. Ford, & D. Deating (eds.), *Advances in applied developmental psychology (Vol. 1) (pp. 1-52).* New York: Academic Press.

Haberman, P.W. (1966). *Childhood symptoms in children of alcoholics and comparison group parents. Journal of Marriage and the Family, 28(2),* 152-154.

Harter, S. (1985). *Manual for the Self-Perception Profile for Children.* University of Denver.

Hegedus, A., Alterman, A., & Tarter, R. (1984). *Learning achievement in sons of alcoholics. Alcoholism: Clinical and Experimental Research, 8(3),* 330-333.

Herjanic, B., & Campbell, W. (1977). *Differentiating psychiatrically disturbed children on the basis of a structured interview. Journal of Abnormal Child Psychology, 5,* 127-134.

Hundleby, J.D. (1987). *Adolescent drug use in a behavioral matrix: A confirmation and comparison of the sexes. Addictive Behaviors, 12,* 103-112.

Hughes, J.M. (1977). *Adolescent children of alcoholic parents and the relationship of Alateen to the children. Journal of Consulting and Clinical Psychology, 45,* 946-947.

Jacob, T., & Leonard, K. (1986). *Psychosocial functioning in children of alcoholic fathers, depressed fathers, and control fathers. Journal of Studies on Alcohol, 47(5),* 373-380.

Jastak, S., & Wilkinson, G.A. (1984). *The Wide Range Achievement Test-Revised.* Wilmington, DE: Jastak Associates.

Jessor, R., & Jessor, S.L. (1977). *Problem Behavior and Psychosocial Development: A Longitudinal Study of Youth.* New York: Academic Press.

Johnson, J.L., & Bennett, L.A. (1988). *School-aged children of alcoholics: Theory and research.* Center of Alcohol Studies Pamphlet Series, Alcohol Research Documentation, Inc, New Brunswick, NJ.

Johnson, J.L., & Rolf, J.E. (1988). *Cognitive functioning in children from alcoholic and non-alcoholic families. British Journal of Addictions, 83,* 849-857.

Johnson, J.L., & Rolf, J.E. (1990). When children change. In: Collins, R.L., Leonard, KE, Searles, JS (eds)., *Alcohol and the Family Research and Clinical Perspectives.* New York, Guilford Press, pp. 162-193.

Johnson, J.L., Sher, K.J., Rolf, J.E. (1991). An overview of models of vulnerability to psychopathology in children of alcoholics. Alcohol, Health, and Research World, 15(1).

Johnson, S., Leonard, K.E., & Jacob, T. (1989). Drinking, drinking styles and drug use in children of alcoholics, depressives and controls. Journal of Studies on Alcohol, 50(5), 427-431.

Kammeier, M.L. (1971). Adolescents from families with and without alcohol problems. Quarterly Journal of Studies on Alcohol, 32(2), 364-372.

Kern, J.C., Hassett, C.A., Collipp, P.J., Bridges, C., Solomon, M., Condren, R.J. (1981). Children of alcoholics: Locus of control, mental age, and zinc level. Journal of Psychiatric Treatment and Evaluation, 3, 169-173.

Knop, J., Teasdale, T., Schulsinger, F., & Goodwin, D. (1985). A prospective study of young men at high risk for alcoholism: School behavior and achievement, Journal of Studies on Alcohol, 46, 273-278.

Kovacs, M. (1983). The children's depression inventory: A self-rated depression scale for school-aged youngsters. (Unpublished manuscript, University of Pittsburgh School of Medicine).

Kovacs, M. & Beck, A.T. (1977). An empirical clinical approach toward a definition of childhood depression. In J.G. Schulterbrandt & A. Raskin (Eds.), Depression in childhood: Diagnosis, treatment, and conceptual models. New York: Raven Press.

Lemoine, P., Harousseau, H., Borteyru, J.P., & Menuet (1968). Children of alcoholic parents: Abnormalities observed in 127 cases. Paris, Ouest Medical, Vol 21, 476-482

Marcus, A.M. (1986). Academic achievement in elementary school children of alcoholic mothers. Journal of Clinical Psychology, 35, 63-78.

Manning, D.T., Balson, P.M., & Xenakis, S. (1986). The prevalence of Type A personality in the children of alcoholics. Alcoholism: Clinical and Experimental Research, 10(2), 184-189.

Miketic, B. (1972). The influence of parental alcoholism in the development of mental disturbances of children. Alcoholism, 8, 135-139.

Miller, D., & Jang, M. (1977). Children of alcoholics: A 20-year longitudinal study. Social Work Research Abstracts, 13(4), 23-29.

Moos, R., & Billings, A. (1982). Children of alcoholics during the recovery process: Alcoholic and matched control families. Addictive Behaviors, 7, 155-163.

Nannis, E.D. (1988). *Cognitive-developmental differences in emotional understanding.* In: Nannis, E.D., and Cowan, P.A. (eds). *Developmental Psychopathology and its Treatment.* San Francisco:Jossey Bass, pp. 31-50.

National Institute on Drug Abuse (1987). *The Adolescent Assessment/ Referral System Manual.* Unpublished manuscript available from L. Rahdert, NIDA, Division of Clinical Research, 5600 Fishers Lane, Room 10A-30, Rockville, MD, 20857.

Nylander, I., & Rydelius, P.A. (1982). *A comparison between children of alcoholic fathers from excellent versus poor social conditions. Acta Paediatrica Scandinavica, 71,* 809-813.

Pandina, R.J., & Johnson, V. (1989). *Familial drinking history as a predictor of alcohol and drug consumption among adolescent children. Journal of Studies on Alcohol, 50(3),* 245-253.

Piaget, J. (1928). *Judgment and Reasoning in the Child.* New York: Harcourt & Brace.

Piaget, J. (1951). *Play, Dreams, and Imitation in Childhood.* New York:Norton.

Piaget, J. (1955). *The Child's Construction of Reality.* New York: Routledge and Kegan Paul.

Piaget, J. (1963). *The Origins of Intelligence in Children.* New York: Norton and Company.

Piaget, J. (1970). *Genetic Epistemology.* New York: Norton and Company.

Plant, M.A., Orford, J., & Grant, M. (1989). *The effects on children and adolescents of parents excessive drinking: An international review. Public Health Records, 104(5),* 433-442.

Prewett, M.J., Spence, R., & Chaknis, M. (1981). *Attribution of Causality by Children with Alcoholic Parents. The International Journal of the Addictions, 16(2),* 367-370.

Reich, W., & Earls, F.J. (1982). *The Home Environment Interview for Children. Child and Parent Versions.* St. Louis, Washington University.

Reich, W., Herjanic, B., Wilner, Z., & Ghandy, P.R. (1982). *Development of a structured psychiatric interview for children. Agreement on diagnosis comparing child and parent interviews. Journal of Abnormal Child Psychology, 10,* 325-336.

Rhodes, J., & Blackham, G.J. (1987). *Differences in character roles* between adolescents from alcoholic and nonalcoholic homes. *American Journal of Drug and Alcohol Abuse, 13(1 & 2)*, 145-155.

Rohrbeck, C.A., Azar, S.T., & Wagner, P.E. (1991). Child self-control rating scale: Validation of a child self-report measure. *Journal of Clinical Child Psychology, 20(2)*, 179-183.
Rolf, J.E., Masten, A.S., Cicchetti, D., Nuechterlein, K.H., Weintraub, S. (1990). *Risk and Protective Factors in the Development of Psychopathology*. New York: Oxford University Press.

Rolf, J., Johnson, J.L., Israel, E., Baldwin, J., & Chandra, A. (1988). Depressive affect in school-aged children of alcoholics. *British Journal of Addiction, 83*, 841-848.

Roosa, M.W., Beals, J., Sandler, I.N., Pillow, D.R. (1990). The role of risk and protective factors in predicting symptomatology in adolescent self-identified children of alcoholic parents. *American Journal of Community Psychology, 18(5)*, 725-741.

Roosa, M.W., Sandler, I.N., Beals, J., & Short, J.L. (1988). Risk status of adolescent children of problem-drinking parents. *American Journal of Community Psychology, 16(2)*, 225-239.

Roosa, M.W., Sandler, I.N., Gehring, M., Beals, J., & Cappo, L. (1988). The Children of Alcoholics Life-Events Schedule: A stress scale of children of alcohol abusing parents. *Journal of Studies on Alcohol, 49(5)*, 422-429.

Rubio-Stipec, M., Bird, H., Canino, G., Bravo, M., & Alegria, M. (1991). Children of alcoholic parents in the community. *Journal of Studies on Alcohol, 52(1)*, 78-88.

Russell, M. (1991). Prevalence of alcoholism among children of alcoholics. In Windle, M., Searles, J.S. (eds) *Children of Alcoholics:Critical Perspectives*. New York:Guilford Press, pp 9-38.

Russell, M., Henderson, C., & Blume, S. (1985). *Children of alcoholics: A review of the literature*. New York: Children of Alcoholics Foundation, Inc.

Rydelius, P.A. (1981). Children of alcoholic fathers: Their social adjustment and their health status over 20 years. *Acta Paediatrica Scandinavica: Supplement 286 to Vol. 70*, 1-89.

Searles, J.S., & Windle, M. (1991). Introduction and overview: Salient issues in the children of alcoholics literature. In: Windle, M., Searles, J.S. (eds). *Children of Alcoholics: Critical Perspectives*, New York:Guilford Press, 1-8.

Sher, K.J. (in press). *Children of Alcoholics*. Chicago:Chicago University Press.

Shurygin, G.I. (1974). Characteristics of the mental development of children of chronic alcoholic mothers. *Pediatriya, VII,* 71-73.

Siegler, R.S., & Jenkins, E. (1989). *How Children Discover New Strategies.* Hillsdale, NJ: Lawrence Erlbaum Ass.
Silverman, W.K., Fleisig, W., Rabian, B., & Peterson, R.A. (1991). Childhood Anxiety Sensitivity Index. *Journal of Clinical Child Psychology, 20(2),* 162-168.

Speilberger, C.D. (1973). State-Trait Anxiety Inventory for Children: Preliminary Manual. Palo Alto, CA: Consulting Psychologists Press.

Steinhausen, H.C., Nestler, V., & Huth, H. (1982). Psychopathology and mental functions in the offspring of alcoholic and epileptic mothers. *Journal of the American Academy of Child Psychiatry, 21(3),* 268-273.

Stern, R., Kendall, A., Eberhard, P. (1991). Children of alcoholics in the schools: Where are they? Their representation in special education. *Psychology in the Schools, 28,* 116-123.

Tarter, R.E. (1990). Evaluation and treatment of adolescent substance abuse: A decision tree method. *American Journal of Drug and Alcohol Abuse, 16(1 & 2),* 1-46.

Tarter, R.E., Jacob, T., & Bremer, D.A. (1989). Cognitive status of sons of alcoholic men. *Alcoholism: Clinical and Experimental Research, 13(2),* 232-235.

Tarter, R.E., Hegedus, A.M., Gavaler, J.S. (1985). Hyperactivity in sons of alcoholics. *Journal of Studies on Alcohol, 46(3),* 259-261.

Tarter, R.E., Hegedus, A., Goldstein, G., Shelly, C., & Alterman, A. (1984). Adolescent sons of alcoholics: Neuropsychological and personality characteristics. *Alcoholism: Clinical and Experimental Research, 8,* 216-222.

Thalinger, D.J. & Kovanek, M.E. (1988). Children of alcoholics-At risk and unserved. A review of research and science roles for school psychologists. *School Psychology Review, 17(1),* 166-191.

von Knorring, A.L. (1991). Annotation: Children of alcoholics. *Journal of Child Psychology and Psychiatry, 32(3),* 411-421.

Warner, R.H., & Rosett, H.L. (1975). The effects of drinking on offspring. *Journal of Studies on Alcohol, 36(11),* 1395-1420.

Watters, T.S., & Theimer, W. (1978). Children of alcoholics: A critical review of some literature. Contemporary Drug Problems, Summer, 195-201.

Werner, E. (1984). Resilient children. Young Children, 40, 68-72.

Werner, E. (1989). High risk children in young adulthood: A longitudinal study from birth to 32 years. American Journal of Orthopsychiatry, 59, 72-81.

Werner, E.E. (1986). Resilient offspring of alcoholics: A longitudinal study from birth to age 18. Journal of Studies on Alcohol, 47, 34-40.

Werner, E.E., & Smith, r.S. (1982). Vulnerable but invincible: A study of resilient children. New York: McGraw-Hill.

West, M.O., & Prinz, R.J. (1987). Parental alcoholism and childhood psychopathology. Psychological Bulletin, 102(2), 204-218.

Whipple, S.C., & Noble, E.P. (1991). Personality Characteristics of alcoholic fathers and their sons. Journal of Studies on Alcohol, 52(4), 331-337.

Wilson, C. & Orford, J. (1978). Children of alcoholics: Report of a preliminary study and comments on the literature. Journal of Studies on Alcohol, 39, 121-142.

Windle, M. (1989). Children of alcoholics: A comprehensive bibliography. New York State Division of Alcoholism and Alcohol Abuse, Research Institute on Alcoholism.

Winters, K.C., & Henly, G.A. (1989). Personal Experience Inventory test and manual. Los Angeles: Western Psychological Services.

Zetterstrom, R., & Nylander, I. (1985). Children in families with alcohol abuse. In: U. Rydberg et al. (Eds). Alcohol and the Developing Brain. New York:Raven Press, 153-159.

Zucker, R.A., & Fitzgerald, H.E. (1991). Early developmental factors and risk for alcohol problems. Alcohol, Health, and Research World, 15(2), in press.

Appendix A

<u>From the child's perspective:</u>

1. Diagnosis

Diagnostic Interview for Children (DICA) (Reich, Herjanic, Wilmer, Ghandy, 1982). This interview elicits psychiatric symptoms in children and adolescents that permit 16 diagnoses to be made according to DSM-III criteria (ADD, oppositional disorder, conduct disorder, alcohol abuse, drug abuse, depression, separation anxiety disorder, over anxious disorder, phobia, gender, identity disorder, anorexia, bulimia, enuresis, encopresis, possible psychosis). There is also a parallel parent version.

2. Home Environment

Home Environment Interview for Children (HEIC) (Reich, Earls, Powell, 1988). This assesses the child's relationships with parents, siblings, relatives, and peers, and involvement in activities in and outside the home environment. It covers the child's school performance, discipline in the home, parents as role models, psychosocial stressors, and relationship to alcoholic parent.

3. Personality

High School Personality Questionnaire (HSPQ) (Cattell et al. 1984). The HSPQ addresses 14 primary personality characteristics.

Junior Eysenck Personality Inventory (Eysenck, 1963). This provides extraversion and neuroticism scales. It also has an adult analog.

4. Self Perception of Competence

Perceived Competence Scale for Children (PCSC) (Harter, 1979). This questionnaire produces six subscales: cognitive, physical, social, academic, global.

5. Academic Performance

Wide Range Achievement Test-Revised (WRAT-R) (Jastak and Wilkinson, 1984). Provides standardized grade level and age-normed percentiles scores for reading, spelling, and arithmetic.

6. Stress

Life Events Questionnaire-Child's Version (LEQ-C) (Garmezy, 1981). The LEQ is a questionnaire designed to measure the child's perception of stress in his/her life.

7. Intellectual Functioning

The Wechsler Intelligence Scale for Children-III or the Wechsler Adult Intelligence Scale-Revised (age 16 and above)

8. Self Perception of Behavior

Youth Self Report (YSR) (Achenbach and Edelbrock, 1987). A self report filled out by 11 to 18 year olds designed to assess competence and behavior problems.

9. Affect

Children's Depression Inventory (CDI) (Kovacs, 1983; Kovacs and Beck, 1977). The CDI is a self report of depression for youths aged 8 to 15.

Beck Depression Inventory (BDI) (Beck and Beck, 1972; Beck and Beamesderfer, 1974). A self report of depression for those aged 16 and older.

From the parent's perspective:

1. Child Behavior Checklist (CBCL) (Achenbach & Edelbrock, 1983). This checklist is comprised of 113 behavior problems and 20 competence items designed to be reported by parents of children ages 4 to 16 years. The items on the CBCL have been factor analyzed separately by sex for the age strata corresponding to preschool, grade school, and high school ages and have been normed according to clinic and non-clinic samples. The CBCL's factoring according to sex and age provides primary and secondary factor T-scores which are interpreted according to their percentile deviations from the reference groups.

2. Life Events Questionnaire-Parent's Version (LEQ-P) (Garmezy, 1981). The LEQ is a questionnaire designed to measure the parent's perception of stress in their child's life.

Small Steps Becoming Large: Effective Strategies to Assist Children of Alcoholics in the Healing Process

by Jerry Moe, MA

For the past eighteen years there has been a growing and encouraging emergence of programs and practitioners to assist youngsters living in alcoholic and other drug addicted families. While prevention continues to lag far behind intervention and treatment, these scattered attempts to reach children, some as young as four, do acknowledge the accepted truth that everyone in the family, <u>especially the children</u>, is adversely impacted by substance abuse. These efforts are also grounded on the hypothesis that significant risk for future addiction may be greatly reduced by working with these children now.

In recent years the scope of these efforts has widened further to include children in other families that also experience the same silence and suffering that children of substance abuse endure. In their families, addiction to food, work, gambling, and relationships, and co-dependency create a similarly stifling environment of tension, fear, isolation, and pain. Youngsters living in violent and abusive households, as well as those in families challenged by mental health problems, often experience similar dynamics.

Despite the huge disparity between the need and what we have been able to provide, the last eighteen years have brought considerable quality and hope to the undertaking, manifested primarily by the wealth of knowledge and understanding we have gained to more effectively assist these youngsters. The evolution of programs, research and effective evaluation methodology have magnified our capacity to empower children and their families in creating a new legacy of health and wellness.

Building Strengths and Resilience

Despite the fact that children from addicted families are at risk for a variety of problems as they grow and develop, research shows the majority of these children become successful, productive, and functioning adults. How did these youngsters beat the odds and overcome adversity? Many children of addiction build a variety of strengths and resilience to successfully cope with the varied challenges they face. Werner, in her longitudinal study, and other researchers have found many traits of resilient individuals, including:

> social competence,
> problem - solving skills,
> the development of autonomy,
> and a sense of purpose and future.

Wolin has cited the importance of family rituals as an important protective factor to assist youngsters.

This growing body of research has created a paradigm shift with a focus on health, wellness, and prevention instead of damage and sickness. While it doesn't deny that children can be scarred by growing up in addicted families, it sheds light on how they can build resilience. Children don't develop these skills in a vacuum, but in the context of creating relationships with nurturing adults. Such relationships can be fostered in family, school, and community settings where such traits as caring and support, high expectations, and active youth participation are all present. Helping youngsters to build these relationships and develop life skills are key to creating that new legacy.

This paper will explore a variety of ways to help children of addiction deepen their strengths and resilience. It will emphasize that proper attention to both the process and the content of our work is essential. Inherent in both of these is, of course, the recruitment and training of people who can successfully implement and facilitate the work. This chapter will state and describe five principles of process that my own experience, and that of others, illuminate as cornerstones to effectively reach these children. It will then take four (of a number of possible) content domain/spheres and provide examples of activities that can be used to exemplify and teach the desired content for those domains. Our work is still so limited as compared to the need that it is essential that we do it effectively. The process principles and the kind of content given as examples here will serve as foundations on which to make the most of the money and resources we have available.

Basic Process Principles

There are many essential ingredients to empowering young children from alcoholic and other high stress families, especially in the group setting. Consistently combining these principles creates an atmosphere conducive to trusting, talking, and feeling. The group setting becomes a safe place for so many who thought they were all alone.

1. Enter the Children's World
2. Create a Safe and Nurturing Environment
3. Beyond Words . . . Experiential Learning
4. Acknowledge Children's Learning Styles with Varied Activities
5. Have Fun

Enter the Children's World

Facilitators may possess the latest tools and techniques yet be rendered fairly ineffective without a "heart to heart" connection with the children. This can only take place if the group leaders enter the children's world by giving them focused attention and love. Sometimes this simple fact is forgotten in the process of getting the job done.

There are many ways to enter the children's world. First of all, facilitators need to be an integral part of group -- if youngsters sit on the floor, so do the facilitators; if youngsters are involved in a self - worth exercise, so are the facilitators. Secondly, it's helpful for facilitators to learn the name of each group participant and call everyone by his or her name. The Children Are People program offers a fun way to accomplish this task by the "Name Game" activity. Children thoroughly enjoy coming up with a fun name beginning with the first letter of their first name. Over the years I've become known as "Jellybeans Jerry" to hundreds of kids. This word association helps facilitators remember names and use them, thereby according the youngsters dignity and respect.

It is also highly helpful for facilitators to know a few things about each participant. The "Share Square" activity will garner important facts as kids respond to such questions as what is their favorite TV show, cartoon character, hobby or game, and reveal a favorite wish. Facilitators can write down the "Name Game" names and fun

brave   kind

smiles alot   # JOSH

caring

shares feelings   smart

a friend

pertinent "Share Square" data on three-by-five cards for easy review and reference before each session. Many children of addiction aren't used to being addressed by their appropriate name and asked questions about meaningful and relevant things in their lives. Above all, it's vital for facilitators to be "real" - i.e. consistently exhibit congruence between what they say and do in group. When facilitators take the time to show they truly care, the "heart to heart" connection deepens. Children don't care about how much adults know until they know about how much adults care.

Create a Safe and Nurturing Environment

Entering the children's world goes a long way to establishing a nurturing environment. Warm, personable, and open facilitators enhance and deepen this process, as youngsters feel cared for and valued in special ways. A basic group structure provides consistency and predictability for children who often live in chaotic and unpredictable environments. Group members derive a certain comfort from this as the safety allows them to take more risks and open up in group. Lastly, clear rules and consistently enforced consequences when the rules get broken establish expectations, limits and boundaries which protect children and deepen the safety that the group offers in an on-going fashion.

Beyond Words . . . Experiential Learning

All too often words have virtually no meaning for youngsters from addicted family systems. "I'll quit tomorrow", "Mommy will be right back", and "If your Dad stays out one more night I'm gonna divorce him", are familiar messages that children hear again and again. Broken promises, inconsistency, and family denial, shrouded in secrecy, can leave children with a strong impression that words are hollow. It is essential to get beyond words in assisting young children of addiction.

When the session began, Jimmy's hand shot into the air to go first. This ten year-old had experimented with many different voices as he spoke through the "Confused Connie" feeling pup-pet. After a few silly comments these words tumbled out of Jimmy's mouth, "Why do men marry women and have kids and say they love the kids only to hit and hurt them?" The group fell silent as Jimmy's eyes filled with tears. Now talking with his own voice he uttered, "I hate Dad when he does that, but I still love him. What's wrong with me?" Jimmy sobbed as the group rallied around him with support and encouragement. He'd taken a huge step in the process of his own recovery.

Instead of merely talking about feelings or addiction (Jimmy had made a breakthrough by using a puppet), facilitators can bring the concepts to life through specially designed games and activities that get kids involved and illustrate key points through the experience. A Chinese proverb says it best :

> *When I hear something, I forget it;*
> *When I see something, I remember it;*
> *When I do something, I understand it.*

Acknowledge Children's Learning Styles With Varied Activities

Youngsters learn in a variety of ways. Some learn best visually, others by ear, and still others kinesthetically. Facilitators can most effectively reach a group of children by utilizing varied activities. These may include skits, art, music, movement, dance, role plays, films, puppets, and "game shows" that stimulate different learning styles. After youngsters have experienced different activities, the ensuing discussion often has added depth and insight.

Have Fun

Many children of addiction grow up way too fast. Some take on adult roles and responsibilities while others shoulder worries, burdens, and concerns which block the spontaneity, joy, magic, and wonder of being a kid. Facilitators can assist youngsters to learn and grow and also provide an opportunity for the children to be kids. By setting a mood which inspires creativity, joy, and laughter, group leaders provide a healing atmosphere conducive to talking, trusting, and feeling. Fun is healing and essential.

These tips can enhance the quality and effectiveness of the group process. Youngsters who feel safe, respected, cared for, and are given the opportunity to feel, learn, and grow in various ways will reach out, take risks, and allow themselves to become vulnerable in miraculous ways. Properly trained facilitators, benefitting from on-going supervision and in-services, are the key to balancing these process principles in a consistent and loving manner (See <u>Conducting Support Groups for Elementary K-6 Children : A Guide for Educators and Other Professionals</u>, Johnson Institute, 1991).

Content Areas

Most groups for young children of addiction utilize an educational support group format. Each session provides specific information on important life skills as well as the support and practice young-sters need to integrate this data into their daily lives. Some children, especially in cases of abuse, abandonment, and other trauma, need much more assistance and guidance than an educational support group offers. Individual therapy may be warranted in such cases.

Educational support groups, usually meeting on a weekly basis, offer a specific theme for each session. While programs across the country feature a variety of topics, including Defenses, Alcohol and Other Drugs, Family, Problem Solving, Risks and Choices, and Making Friends, both research and experience point to four content areas critical to helping children from addicted family systems.

1. Feelings (All my feelings are okay)
2. Alcohol, Other Drugs and Addiction (It's not my fault)
3. Self - Care (It's important to take care of myself)
4. Self - Worth (I am special)

The rest of this paper will explore these content areas and feature a specially designed game or activity relevant to each.

Feelings

Many children of addiction survive by learning not to feel. The prospect of talking, let alone sharing feelings, can raise young-sters' guilt and anxiety, as they fear betraying their parents and the family secrets. A small group often serves as the first safe place they have ever had to be open and explore feelings. Children learn that all feelings are okay. Group becomes a safety net where youngsters deepen their skills in identifying, expressing, and owning their feelings. "Stuffed Feelings and Problems" is an activity which facilitates this process.

"Stuffed Feelings and Problems" is a kinesthetic experience which helps children understand the consequences of holding problems and feelings inside. With the group sitting in a circle, the facilitators place a tote bag, full of brightly colored rocks, in the middle. Each rock has a problem (such as "addiction". "depression", "co-dependency", and "family secrets") or a feeling (such as "anger", "scared", "hurt", "shame", "guilty", and "sad") painted on it. One by one the youngsters pick up the bag and carry it around the room. The facilitators ask, "How does it feel carrying all this stuff?", or "Can you be free to be a kid and laugh and play when you've got that bag with you?", and "When you carry such a heavy load what are you often thinking about?".

After a brief discussion, the facilitators put the bag back in the middle of the circle. Each child takes a rock out of the bag and reads the problem or feeling on the rock. They then have the opportunity to share a time when they felt that feeling or had that particular problem. Group members quickly come to see that they are not alone; everyone has problems and feelings. Before long the bag is empty, and everyone has the chance to carry it around again. There is amazement at how much lighter it is because they talked about their problems and feelings -- they got them out. The facilitators explain that this is the actual function and work of group -- to better understand problems by talking about them and to share feelings to let go of their weight and intensity. Afterward, young children often say, "You let go of a couple more rocks today!", after a group member has disclosed a particularly tough problem and shared his or her painful feelings.

Addiction

Youngsters living in addicted families may be confused about what is going on in a home often shrouded in silence and secrecy. Educational support groups can help youngsters learn about addiction, especially that it's not their fault and they are not alone, in age appropriate ways. It is essential to help children differentiate themselves from their parent's problems and realize they didn't cause the problems and can't make them better. There are

many excellent stories, films, and activities[1] which bring this cunning and baffling disease to within understanding for children. Music can also be effective in deepening youngsters' grasps of the problem and encouraging them to freely express their feelings toward addiction and its manifestations.

During my years as a teacher, I was amazed by kids who couldn't remember their multiplication tables yet could sing Michael Jackson's song "Beat It" forwards, backwards, and side-ways. Music is a universal language that can deeply touch the human soul. An effective way to incorporate music is to take popular rock or rap melodies and have the group re-write the lyrics (over 2 - 3 sessions) to describe their experiences in living with addiction, and/or a variety of ways to positively cope with it. Once youngsters have already learned some basic facts about alcohol-ism, this powerful activity helps them unlock problems and feel-ings, as well as deepen their understanding about addiction and its impact on them. For example, a group of three twelve- year olds and their facilitator spent time rewriting the lyrics to Elton John's "I Guess That's Why They Call It the Blues". First they listened to the song a few times and studied a copy of the lyrics handed out to each of them. Then through dialogue, debate, and collabora-tion, "I Guess That's Why I'm Always Confused" was born and became a theme song for the Children's Program (see example). Group members sometimes sing it to newcomers as a way of communicating their common bond and the hope for health and recovery.

Self - Care

Telling young children of addiction to take good care of them-selves is largely a futile exercise, like speaking to them in a foreign language. Remember, they live in families without many role models of self-care. Kids need "maps" on this important life skill and lots of practice to integrate it into their daily lives. "Jeopardy, The Self - Care Game", in conjunction with "Self - Care Bags", go a long way in imparting this skill in a fun and balanced manner.

"Jeopardy, The Self - Care Game", is a take-off on the popular television game show, here with an emphasis on taking good care of one's self. (If you don't take good care of yourself, you really

JEOPARDY

SELF-CARE GAME

BODY

-
-
-

MIND

-
-
-

FEELINGS

-
-
-

SPIRIT

-
-
-

BEING A KID

-
-
-

are in jeopardy!) With the Jeopardy categories of "Body", "Mind", "Feelings", "Spirit", and "Being a Kid" written on newsprint or a blackboard, the facilitator records the group's brainstormed responses in each important area. For example, "Exercise is a way to take care of your body." The activity continues until there are many useful ideas for all the categories.

After a brief discussion on the importance of self-care, the facilitators pass out lunch bags and instruct the kids to creatively decorate their bags with their name and the words "self-care bag" by using crayons, colored pencils, and magic markers. The group leader then hands each youngster six index cards and tells them to write one self-care strategy on each side of the cards. Children may utilize the results from "Jeopardy, The Self - Care Game", or further brainstorm ideas on taking good care of themselves. They jot down self-care ideas for their bodies, minds, feelings, spirits, and the "little kids" inside. Then everyone puts their cards in their bags, shakes up the contents and pulls out a card. With a suggestion on each side, youngsters quickly learn they have choices about how to take care of themselves. In each subsequent session, the kids practice self-care by pulling a card from their bags and carrying out the suggestion. At the final group, youngsters brainstorm how to use their bags at home -- for example, when they're bored or not feeling good about themselves, it is helpful to take a card and follow its instructions. Self-care bags teach and allow children to practice taking good care of the most important people of all -- themselves.

Self - Worth

Young children of addiction can get so enmeshed in the negative messages and put-downs of their environments that they believe they have little to celebrate. Some learn to cling to limited self-value based solely on doing, and most sadly, miss out on celebrating their intrinsic beauty and worth. "Living Cards" help children begin to fill this void and touch upon their special and unique gifts.

After participants have creatively written their names in the middle of a piece of paper, they silently reflect upon the special qualities each of the others brings to the group. The facilitators

SHARE
FEELINGS

PLAY A
GAME

SELF-
CARE
BAG

READ

TALK TO
A FRIEND

EXERCISE

may provide a few examples to initiate the flow of ideas, and then record the group's responses on the board in full view for all participants to see and hopefully use in this exercise. The children then pass their paper to the left, and their neighbors write brief notations describing the special qualities of the person whose name is on the sheet. The process continues until each paper circles the room and comes back to the owner. Then follows a full minute of silence called "finding the buried treasure", as each kid reads and absorbs all the special things written about him or her. Everyone has the opportunity to share his or her Living Card with the group. Amidst clapping and cheering, everybody takes a moment to celebrate their special gifts.

It's important now to celebrate the progress made to help young children of addiction in the past eighteen years. Paying close attention to both the process and content of this work can greatly improve quality services for children. While there's still much to do, there's more hope and help available for children today than in the past. There are highly skilled practitioners, books and age-appropriate games and activities that can deeply touch young-sters. Above all else, it's the relationship you develop with chil-dren, not the activities or games, that can make the greatest difference in their lives. One young girl, Jenna, embodies the hope for these children and speaks to the value of early preven-tion and intervention.

Every morning Jenna, age 11, delivers over 200 newspapers. Every cent she earns went to help make ends meet for her family -- a little brother and a mom addicted to alcohol and cocaine. After Family Week at Sierra Tucson's Children's Program, Jenna's mom put a portion of Jenna's monthly earnings in a college savings account and let her keep some spending money for herself. All week in the Children's Program, Jenna kept hearing the importance of taking care of yourself first. Her counselor asked her to go out and buy something just for herself when she got home. Three weeks later Jenna called the counselor. She had decided to buy herself ice cream , yet stood frozen outside the store for twenty minutes. "I didn't want to go in because I thought of all the other things I could do with the money -- cookies for my brother or a nice card for my mom", she told the counselor. Finally Jenna ordered a double dip, ate one scoop and threw the rest away. "I didn't think I really deserved it."

Jenna took a big step that day. She's since bought many double dip cones and eaten them right down to the final bite.

There is much hope today for young children of addiction. With the love and guidance of skilled facilitators and quality programs the children's small steps become large in changing their own legacies. They can hope for a beautiful today and a brighter tomorrow.

I Guess That's Why I'm Always Confused

Just wish it away
Don't look at it
Pretend it's all better
My parents can't stop
I can honestly say they just never get better
Booze and drugs always stay
To cast their demons inside
And it won't be long before Mom and Dad go to
their crazy place
It's time to hide

And I guess that's why I'm always confused
Scared, all alone, and verbally abused
Parents are children
Fighting not hugging
Exploding like thunder
Under their drugging
I guess that's why I'm always confused

Just stare into space
I've been disgraced
Friends just don't understand
Live for each second
With pained reservations and
Never count on parent's plans
It's just no use
Cry in the night if it helps
Yet nothing helps
It seems they love booze
More than they love me or life itself

I guess that's why I'm always confused
Scared, all alone, and verbally abused
Parents are children
Fighting not hugging
Forgetting their loved ones
Under their drugging
and I guess that's why I'm always confused

References

Disrupted Family Rituals: A Factor in the Intergenerational Transmission of Alcoholism. **Wolin, Bennett, Noonan, et. al., Journal of Studies on Alcohol. 41: 199-214, 1980.**

Children Are People Support Group Manual. *Health Communications, Deerfield Beach, Florida, 1988.*

Conducting Support Groups for Elementary Children K - 6 : A Guide for Educators and Other Professionals. Jerry Moe and Peter Ways. Johnson Institute, Minneapolis, Minnesota, 1991.

Kids' Power : Healing Games for Children of Alcoholics. Jerry Moe and Don Pohlman. Health Communications, Deerfield Beach, Florida, 1989.

Overcoming the Odds: High Risk Children From Birth to Adulthood. Werner and Smith. Cornell University Press, Ithaca, New York, 1992.

All activities in this paper are taken from

Discovery . . . Finding the Buried Treasure : A Prevention / Intervention Program for Youth from High Stress Families. Jerry Moe. STEM Publishing, Tucson, Arizona, 1993.

[1]*See* **Kids' Power : Healing Games for Children of Alcoholics**, *Health Communications, 1989.*

Matching Services and the Needs of Children of Alcoholic Parents: A Spectrum of Help

Ellen R. Morehouse, ACSW, NCAC II

Introduction

Young and adolescent COAs experience a wide range of effects resulting from a parent's alcoholism. While the vast majority of studies of COAs identify the negative impact of parental alcoholism on children, a growing number of studies have begun to document the factors that contribute to the absence of these negative effects. Clearly, COAs who have been provided with protective factors, appear more resilient, and function well, do not need the same kinds of services as COAs who are experiencing the most negative consequences of a parent's alcoholism. Therefore, services to COAs must be appropriate to the needs of the child, enhance or stimulate protective factors, and reduce the negative consequences when they exist.

This article will examine the range of services for COAs, the settings where they are and can occur, the effectiveness of these services, and the service gaps that exist. Suggested ingredients for services and criteria for matching the needs of the child to the type of service and the setting will be provided. The training, qualifications, and supervision of those who work with COAs will also be discussed.

Historical Perspective

Historically, COAs received services for problems that were caused by a parent's alcoholism in settings that dealt with the child's symptom, such as the school phobia or acting out behavior, rather than the cause of the problem. A 1974 study by Booz Allen Hamilton for NIAAA [1] looked at these services and found that, although these children have access to support systems such as schools, churches, physicians, extended families, social agencies, and specialized services, "there are gaps between the needs of the child and the actual resources available; these involve non-responsiveness, inadequate coverage, ineffectiveness, and failure to identify such children." Some believe that this landmark study combined with the growing popularity of the family therapy and prevention movements in the 1970s stimulated the development of services designed specifically for COAs.

Results of studies on the effects of parental alcoholism on COAs were published throughout the 1970s and services for COAs in schools and in alcoholism treatment programs were being provided in 1974. But by 1979, there was recognition and concern by NIAAA that despite the well documented needs, services were not being provided to meet the demand. [2] As a result, a two day symposium was sponsored by NIAA in September 1979. "The purpose of the symposium was to have a representative sample of professionals providing COA-specific services, share experiences and insights, identify critical policy issues, and assess future needs." [3] The Symposium resulted in a monograph published in 1981 titled Services for Children of Alcoholics. This monograph identified some of the barriers to providing services that still exist today. It also documented how programs were successfully able to overcome these barriers and provide services to COAs.

A 1986 publication of the Children of Alcoholics Foundation, Directory of National Resources for Children of Alcoholics, [4] lists 259 programs that provide direct services specifically designed to serve COAs. Of these programs, 145 serve children under 18. (Programs which treat COAs as part of a larger population but which were not specifically designed for COAS and programs requiring a parent to be in a particular alcoholism treatment program in order for the child to receive services were not included.)

Current Situation

Despite the significant increase in COA-specific services since 1979, it is estimated that only a small percentage of all COAs participate in these services. A 1991 study by Student Assistance Services of the reasons why COAs don't participate in COA services outside the school found that the 10 most common reasons given by adolescent COAs were:

1. "I don't want my parents to know."
2. "I can't get there" (because of transportation or because of location).
3. "I can't afford it."
4. "Trust. I don't want to share my problems with strangers."
5. "It's not that bad" or "I can handle it myself."
6. " I don't have time to go."
7. Embarrassment.
8. Fear of revealing the secret, told not to tell.
9. "I'm not crazy!" Afraid of stigma.
10. "I don't want my friends to know."

Other reasons cited include: "I tried Alateen and didn't feel comfortable," "I tried counseling and it wasn't helpful," "It's not my problem, Why should I have to go?", "I don't want to lie to my parents" and "It won't help".

These results indicate a need to provide services in different kinds of settings and a need to prepare adolescents for services.

With COAs accounting for approximately 13% of all children and adolescents in this country, an argument can be made to 1) train all professionals who work with youth in the basics of how to help COAs and how to locate more intensive services for them; and to 2) train COA specialists who can provide treatment to COAs and consultation to their professional colleagues or staff in non-COA-specific settings, such as youth centers, mental health clinics, schools; and to 3) establish more COA-specific services in host settings as well as in free standing programs.

BARRIERS TO SERVICE

Parent Consent

Many states have laws requiring parents' consent for medical, mental health, and alcohol and drug treatment for minors. As a result, many organizations that are willing to serve COAs require parent consent.[5] While this is not usually a barrier for COAs with recovering parents, it is often a barrier for COAS with active alcoholic parents for the following reason: First, many active alcoholics deny that they have a problem with alcohol and drugs, and deny that the drinking has negatively affected their children. Some recovering alcoholics also have difficulty acknowledging the negative impact of their drinking on the children because of the high degree of guilt that is generated. The non-using parent may also deny the negative consequences on the children because of guilt. Both parents may deny the negative impact because they may believe that the child doesn't know the parent has a drinking problem. This is illustrated through statements such as "He never drank in the house" or "The children think mom sleeps a lot because she works so hard," etc.

Second, even when denial is not the issue, some parents do not want their children involved in services because of fear that there will be a violation of privacy and the child and family might then be stigmatized and treated differently by others. This is characterized by statements such as "If my child attends that program and someone sees her walk in the door, then everyone in town will know." Despite the increasing acceptance of alcoholism as a disease, there is still a high degree of prejudice. A well known professional in the alcoholism field who is open about her own recovery acknowledges that her 12 year old daughter has a friend who is not allowed to play or sleep at her house yet is regularly invited to the friend's home. The friend told her daughter that this is because "your mom could have a relapse."

The child's and parent's fear of stigmatization has not been given adequate consideration by service providers. This issue can be addressed by providing COA-specific services in non-stigmatiz-ing or generic settings and by instituting internal procedures to protect privacy. For example, a school social worker who learns that the reason a child is having a lot of problems with school is a result of the alcoholic mother's actions, can still give input into a team decision (child study team, Committee on Special Education, etc.) without identifying the alcoholism. This can by done by saying "Lisa" is having a hard time because her mother was absent alot, was having medical problems, provided inconsistent parenting, etc. By describing the actions of the mother and how they affect "Lisa", the team can plan what actions are needed without stigmatizing the mother. Many parents fear that they and their children are gossiped about in the faculty lunch room.

A third reason why parents may not consent is because they need the child to perform parenting tasks that may not be accomplished if the child attends an out-of-school program. Statements such as "You can't go to that program after school because I need you to watch your sister for me, work that part-time job, etc." are examples of this kind of thinking. This thinking would make it difficult to attend any after school or weekend program regardless of the location.

Family Focus

Many programs for children and adolescents insist on parent involvement and don't service youth without parent involvement. While there is general agreement in the youth services field that services to children and youth will be most effective when the parents are involved, parent involvement is not always possible or desirable, especially when providing services to COAs. For example, many children would be punished if they told the parent they wanted help. Others would be forbidden from attending services. Therefore, programs that require parent involvement automatically limit which COAs can attend.

The impact that services without parent participation can have on children should not be underestimated. Services that help COAs develop characteristics that will serve as protective factors for the child are invaluable. Testimonials from adolescents and adults about that person "who made a difference" are well known.

I'm considering the degree of family involvement. It is also important to consider the developmental stage of the child. Specifically with "separation" being one of the primary tasks of adolescent development, it is appropriate that an adolescent may not want any parent involvement in his or her treatment.

It is also important to consider that when a parent is still actively drinking, a child might appropriately not trust that it is safe to share feelings in a family session and fear reprisals from siblings or parents. Similarly, for a young child who has lived with the "don't talk" rule,[6] the child may not understand how, just because dad is in treatment and not drinking, it is now "ok" to talk. The young child may need several to many sessions to develop trust of the counselor/therapist before trusting a conjoint session. Finally, the treatment needs of the child may conflict with the needs of the parent. The most extreme example would be in treating a COA who has been repeatedly sexually abused by an alcoholic parent; no one would argue that the child should only be seen if the parent agrees to be treated.

SETTINGS FOR SERVICES FOR COAs

COA-specific services are most commonly provided in the following settings:

Schools

The CASPAR Alcohol Education in Massachusetts was the first documented program to provided COA-specific services in elementary and junior high school. [7] Services were provided through an alcohol education curriculum which included specific material about COAs and training for teachers on how to identify and help COAs. The CASPAR program also provided after-school homogeneous groups for COAs and heterogeneous groups that included COA-specific material. Since CASPAR, a number of other in-school curriculums have been developed that include COA-specific information. Teacher training on COA issues has grown dramatically as has in-school individual and group counseling sessions for COAs.

The Westchester, NY Student Assistance Program was the first documented model for providing professional counselors (called Student Assistance Counselors) in secondary schools for the purpose of working specifically with COAs.[8] In this model assessment, individual and group counseling, and referral of COAs are conducted during school by these specialists.

With the growing knowledge and acceptance of the needs of COAs, schools have provided COA-awareness activities for all students. These include poster contests on how alcoholism affects families, assemblies with skits/plays about alcoholic families, library displays with books about COAs, etc.

These activities are critical because they reduce the isolation felt by many COAs by letting them know that there are many other students with family alcoholism. They also do this without singling anyone out and therefore, reduce or eliminate the barriers discussed earlier. The biggest advantage of in-school programs are accessibility and in many instances, parent notification isn't required.

Alcoholism Treatment Programs

Most alcoholism treatment programs today have a family education component to help the family understand alcoholism and recovery. Many also provide support and counseling for the family members. Programs of this kind fall into two categories. The first includes programs where the children attend only if the parent or parenting figure is receiving treatment. When the parent ends treatment the child(ren) end(s) treatment. These types of programs can be thought of as COA collateral programs because the primary patient is the adult. In these programs, the length of the child's participation can range from one session to an unlimited number of sessions. The parent can be in an in-patient program and the child comes for out-patient visits, or the child may stay over during family week, or both can be outpatients. The biggest advantage of these programs is that the child has the parent's permission to attend and therefore feels less guilt about talking about the situation at home.

The second category of programs for COAs in alcoholism treatment is where the COA is the primary client/patient and is provided services regardless of the parent(s) involvement. For example, in New York State COAs may be treated in alcoholism treatment programs for their COA issues without parental consent if the professional thinks that parent notification would not be in the child's best interest. In programs where the COA is the primary client/patient, services tend to be more tailored to the developmental needs of the individual child. The biggest advantage of these programs is that, like in-school counseling programs, the child's participation is not contingent on the parent.

Free Standing COA Programs

Project Rainbow, started in 1979, was the first free standing program providing COA-specific services. Since then, others have developed around the country. Most of these programs provide services during non-school hours and are offered after school, weekend, and during the summer. Most contain a recreation component as well and last for several hours. The biggest advantages of these programs are that they offer more opportunities for socialization and fun for the children while providing help, and offer the most opportunity for the child to be out of the dysfunctional family system.

Other COA-specific Services

Other COA-specific services operate in a wide variety of settings. A common setting is the private practice where an individual practitioner or group of practitioners offer COA-specific services as part of the private practice. A growing number of child guidance clinics, family agencies and out-patient mental health clinics also provide COA-specific individual and/or group counseling for COAs. These programs offer the advantage of staff with experience in diagnosing and treating the broad range of child and adolescent psychiatric disorders. Therefore, a COA who also has an attention deficit disorder with hyperactivity and is depressed might best be treated in this kind of setting.

Youth programs such as Boys Clubs, "Ys", community centers, sometimes also offer COA-specific services. Perhaps the biggest advantage of these programs is the lack of stigma attached to participation. With these programs, a child can attend to play basketball, do arts and crafts, or talk.

Examples of crisis programs that can provide COA-specific services are programs for runaway and homeless youth, shelters for battered women and children, and rape crisis centers. These programs provide a window of opportunity to address COA issues because of the crisis. An adolescent reluctant to talk about an alcoholic father may be motivated to do so because of the fight he had with his drunken father that resulted in being thrown out of the house or in running away.

Councils on Alcoholism also offer COA-specific services, such as alcohol education programs for children, i.e. the BABES program started by the Detroit affiliate of the National Council on Alcoholism, and COA counseling groups.

Residential Child Care/Juvenile Justice Facilities

Many children under 19 are living in group homes or institutional settings. A large portion of these children are COAs yet rarely are involved in COA-specific services. The Berkshire Farm Center in Canaan, N.Y. was the first program to document COA services in a juvenile justice facility in 1984. [9] Since then Student Assistance Services, through an OSAP High Risk Youth Grant, has built on the Berkshire experience and provides COA-specific services in a variety of residential facilities for youth. Two of the unique problems encountered were the residents' reluctance to disclose the extent of the parental alcoholism, fearing that they would not be allowed to return home if the staff knew "how bad" home was; and second, the reluctance to disclose in a COA group because of fear that a member who lives in the facility with him would bring up what was said outside the group. With these COAs, more individual sessions were needed to establish trust before COAs were willing to join a COA group.

RANGE OF COA-SPECIFIC SERVICES

COA-specific services can be viewed on a continuum with awareness raising activities that can benefit everyone on one end to intensive psychotherapy that is only needed by some COAs on the other end of the continuum.

Awareness

Each type of service has different goals. Awareness activities, such as public service announcements (PSAs), print advertisements, posters, book displays, etc., let COAs know they are not alone. They help COAs understand that there are many children with parents who drink too much; that many of these parents do what their parent does, i.e. break promises, or embarrass the child; that many children feel like they do sometimes, i.e. angry, ashamed, scared, etc.; and that there are adults who can help children.

These activities and messages are critical because they break the "don't talk" rule. In most alcoholic families, children are told not to talk about the parents' drinking so they are reluctant to tell outsiders and often other family members about upsetting incidents caused by the alcoholic, or their resulting feelings. As a result, young children especially often believe that what is happening to them is unique. Public awareness activities aimed at youth universalizes their experience and reduces some of the isolation, shame, and confusion.

Education

Education goes a step further by explaining why parents break promises, act differently when drinking, feel and act sick when not drinking, forget things, etc. To be effective, education must fit the cognitive development and learning style of each child. For example, not considering a child's cognitive and emotional development could have a very negative impact when explaining how alcoholism tends to "run in families." Explaining blackouts as a reason for broken promises and forgetfulness would be done very differently for a four year old than for a 14 year old. In providing education, consideration must be given to the fact that some children become highly anxious during this time and may not absorb and integrate the information. Others may have learning disabilities that make it difficult to listen and learn in groups, to read or to write stories, or draw pictures about their feelings or family. In addition, the child's level of moral development (as described by Kolberg[10]) or gender (which affects moral development as described by Gilligan[11]) should also be considered.

Just as awareness can help reduce the isolation, education can help reduce the pain. Understanding that a child is not responsible for the parents' drinking or other activities, that drinking can make it hard for a parent to take care of a child, and that drinking may cause a parent to do things that make a child feel unloved, etc can help a child separate her/himself from the parent's problem. The ability to do this was one of the protective factors identified in Beardslee's study of resilient children of parents with affective disorders.[12] The importance of detaching from the parent's drinking problem has been a long-recognized principle of Alateen. Education is provided in Alateen, and in books, booklets, and movies about COAs. It should be a part of all alcohol education curriculums and COA-specific services.

Education can be provided without identifying or singling out COAs. For example, during COA awareness week, a teacher can assign a book report on one of five articles, books, or booklets on COAs. This allows COAs as well as non-COAs to benefit.

Support for Alcohol Specific Concerns

Giving COAs an opportunity to talk about their situation, listening, and expressing empathy is important because for many COAs, it is not permissible to talk about their situation at home. For those that might try, they often feel no one is listening, or they are told their feelings are wrong. Statements by non-alcoholic spouses such as "You shouldn't feel that way," "Grow up," "You don't know what it means to be upset," "Stop crying or I'll give you something to cry about" are characteristic of parent responses often given to COAs who do express feelings. As a result, many COAs learn it is not safe or wise to express feelings.

Obviously COAs must be identified to receive support for alcohol-specific concerns. The benefits to be gained from receiving support must be compared to the risks of identification in any given setting, and for any COA, in deciding whether or not to participate in this level of services. Support is provided in Alateen and in all individual and group counseling for COAs.

Coping Strategies

The next level of services involves examining how a child is coping with the parent's (s') drinking and resulting behavior, evaluating the efficacy of the strategy, exploring new strategies, and trying them out. The goal of this level of services is behavioral change and/or support for maintaining healthy behaviors. Examples include: learning not to talk back to an intoxicated parent as a way of avoiding punishment; learning that it is normal and healthy to want to go away to college or join the armed services after high school; and learning to draw or call a friend when upset.

While coping strategies are provided in books and booklets, individual and/or group counseling provide a more effective forum.

Often there is resistance from service providers in offering this level of service to COAs because of possible conflicts between what is in the best interests of the child and the parent's wishes. The following case examples illustrate this conflict:

> Mrs. Jones and her eight year old son, Tim, were abandoned by Mr. Jones, Tim's father. Mrs. Jones began alcoholism treatment and was lonely and depressed. She looked forward to Tim's arrival after school to keep her company. She let Tim know that he was a great help to her and was now the "man of the house." Tim realized how much his mom depended on him and avoided any out of school activities with peers so he could "help" his mother. Tim was seen individually in the children's program at the clinic his mother was attending. He admitted wanting to attend after school activities with his friends but felt it would hurt his mother if he wasn't with her after school. As a result, he used every opportunity at school to socialize with friends and got into trouble for talking during class, during assemblies, and at other times when he was supposed to be quiet.
>
> When it was suggested to Mrs. Jones that Tim participate in cub scouts and after school activities she was resistant, admitting that she needed Tim's company and help. How hard to push for what was in Tim's interest raised questions between Tim's counselor and Mrs.Jones' counselor. If they pushed for Tim's interests, would Mrs. Jones drop out of treatment and relapse? If this happened, would the benefits of participation in peer activities outweigh the consequences of Mrs. Jones' drinking? Would Tim stay in these activities if his mother returned to drinking?, etc.

The second example is of seventeen year old Carmen who had an alcoholic father.

> Carmen's home life was unbearable for her. She hated her verbally abusive father and her mother who made her feel guilty for not helping out more at home. Carmen was an honor student who wanted to get away from her family as quickly as possible. She was able to graduate from high school in three years and was accepted with a full scholarship to a very prestigious university far from her home. Her parents wanted her to attend the local community college so she could live at home and help out. Carmen was furious at her parents for trying to keep her at home. She felt she had the right to go to the university and wasn't going to let her parents stop her. She wanted support from her counselor for her decision and information about how to become an emancipated minor. Her parents saw the counselor as interfering and supporting Carmen's disobedience.

These two examples illustrate the underlying issues in the parent consent and family involvement policies. While states have established limits on parent rights (parents don't have the right to abuse or neglect children), clinical practice often is caught between what is best for the child and the rights of the parents. This dilemma often emerges in helping COAs with coping strategies and especially in providing concrete services.

Therapy

Therapy differs from counseling in intensity and in uncovering blocks to adopt healthy coping strategies. Therapy may be short term or long term and reflect a variety of theoretical orientations, such as family systems, psychoanalytic, behavioral, cognitive, etc. Theoretically, therapy is a treatment for a problem, which implies that the COA involved in therapy is having a problem that needs to be remedied. The problem may be the child's unhappiness or the unhappiness of others that results from the child's behavior, such as stealing, fighting, etc. Therapy for COAs should include each of the other levels of service. As with the other levels, be appropriate for the developmental level of the child. Therapy should also improve functioning in areas where the child is having difficulty, such as social functioning, functioning at school, etc.

MATCHING SERVICES TO COAS

Any COA may need any and all levels of services at any given time. For example, an elementary child may benefit from awareness and education and not want a more intensive level of service because "I'm OK." If the situation at home deteriorates, the child may need additional services. Similarly, the situation may improve, but years later as an adolescent the child may begin experiencing flashbacks of beatings, sexual abuse, or other trauma that occurred and that was repressed. At this time the child may begin to deteriorate and need additional services.

While all young COAs can benefit from the first three levels of service (awareness, education, support), a thorough assessment should be done before providing coping strategies and/or therapy. One of the well meaning mistakes often made in the early days of the COA services movement was to force young and adolescent COAs into treatment so they could avoid the problems of adult COAs. A child who thought "everything is OK" was labeled as in denial. This attitude ignores important concepts. First, parental alcoholism is extremely variable. It can be from short to long duration, mild to severe, and accompanied by an extreme range of behaviors that can affect children. Mitigating factors, such as the child's constitutional factors, and the presence of other caretaking and nurturing adults will greatly influence the child's experience of parental alcoholism. Therefore, when some children say "it's not that bad" or "I can handle it," they may be accurate.

Second, denial is usually viewed as a negative defense in the alcoholism field because it perpetuates the drinking. However, for a child, denial can be a positive defense that provides psychic protection for survival. In this situation, it is important to remember that defenses serve a purpose. Forcing a child to give up a defense before he or she is ready can result in regression to a more primitive defense. In other words, children and adolescents should not be forced to participate in COA-specific treatment. An adolescent who tries Alateen several times and does not want to continue should not be made to do so—just as an adult COA who reads a book for COAs and finds it too painful to continue should not be forced to continue reading.

INGREDIENTS OF COA-SPECIFIC SERVICES

All COA-specific services should help COAs understand the following four points:

1. You are not alone. There are many other children with alcoholic parents, who experience what you experience, and feel like you do.
2. You are not responsible for your parent's drinking, alcoholism, behavior, or recovery.
3. You can get help for yourself so things will be better.
4. There are people who can help you.

Counseling in general is based on the premise that "For me to help you, you need to trust me and talk about your feelings"-- three things that are difficult for COAs to do. Therefore, it is necessary to modify standard counseling techniques. It is suggested that this can be done by having the service provider break the "don't talk" rule first by demonstrating an understanding of how parental alcoholism can affect children.[13] This can be done verbally or with reading materials or visual aids, such as pictures or films. The most common concerns and experiences of COAs should be addressed. These include:

1. Children feel responsible, directly or indirectly, for their parent's drinking.
2. Children equate their parent's drinking with not being loved.
3. Children feel angry with the non-alcoholic parent for not protecting them or for causing the alcoholic's drinking.
4. Children fear that the alcoholic will get hurt, sick or die.
5. Children are embarrassed by the parent's inappropriate behavior which can include criminal or sexual behavior.
6. Children never know what to expect because of the inconsistency.
7. Children are confused by the difference between "dry" behavior and "drunk" behavior.
8. Children sometimes want their parents to drink and then feel guilty.

By stating "Here are some of the concerns of other children who have parents who drink too much sometimes", the counselor demonstrates that many situations or feelings are shared by other children. By recognizing that their situation/feelings are not unique, the COA feels less embarrassed to self disclose and more confident that the counselor will understand.

In describing the common concerns listed above, the counselor should take time to provide concrete examples of each concern. Once this has occurred the counselor can ask, "do you have any of these concerns or do any of these situations occur in your house?"

Next, the child should then be given the opportunity to talk. Some may just nod silently, some may ventilate, some may acknowledge they have some of the concerns, while others may deny those concerns, and some may become so anxious they are unable to sit still. If the child does share, the counselor should listen carefully to what the child is most concerned about and ask questions that determine the extent of the impact of the parent's drinking on the child. It is in this step that the assessment should occur.

The third step in counseling COAs is to provide education. This can be done verbally, but articles, books, booklets, and films should be used as a supplement because the COA's anxiety often prevents absorbing the information.

The fourth step of counseling is to provide coping strategies. This should include the opportunity to role play difficult situations and evaluate the efficacy of different strategies.

The fifth step includes examining the child's adaptation to the parent's drinking, the child's comfort or discomfort with their own behavior, and acknowledging that they have choices in how they react to the parent. Often COAs don't see their "problem behavior" as a reaction to the parent. Once they do, they can begin to choose and then develop alternative healthier ways of coping.

The final step is examining blocks to healthier functioning. Treatment of COAs should help them to understand how their past and current family situation affect them and empower them to make the best of the current situation and positively influence the future. For example, an adolescent, who is always hurt by peer relationships because she/he is looking for nurturing that is not provided by the parent, can understand how she/he has unrealistic expectations of friends, becomes hurt, and then keeps people from getting close. This adolescent can learn to identify what are her/his needs, who can meet different needs, how to get the needs met, and then learn what are realistic expectations in different relationships.

OTHER SERVICE ISSUES

When the Parent Becomes Abstinent

Often providers of services to COAs forget that things don't automatically improve for the child, and sometimes get worse when the parent stops drinking. Services for COAs whose parents are abstinent are just as necessary as services to children of actively drinking alcoholic parents. The ingredients of services to children of abstinent/recovering alcoholic parents (CORAs) are similar to those of active alcoholics but in addition they need:

- education about the recovery process
- to re-examine their survival role
- other people to talk with to validate experiences, perceptions, and feelings
- counseling on how to argue with parents and express negative feelings
- to re-examine the impact of the parent on their own behavior

Absent Parents

COAs, whose parents have died or are alive but not living with the child, should also be eligible for COA-specific services because they can still be negatively affected by the parent. Guilt stemming from feeling may be if the child did something different the parent would still be alive or living with the child are common. Anger for being abandoned or guilt that a hated parent is no longer around are also common.

Holidays

Birthdays, religious holidays, and national holidays are supposed to be times for happy celebrations involving the family. Beginning in preschool, children are taught about and celebrate holidays. For many COAs, holidays are the times of great stress and sadness. All services to COAs should be providing holiday specific aware-ness, education, support, and coping strategies for COAs. This includes acknowledging that holidays aren't always happy and are often disappointing, helping COAs prepare for the disappointment, developing alternative celebrations, and realistic expectations. For example, a COA who anticipates that it will be too painful to stay in the house with the family on Thanksgiving can make plans to volunteer to serve meals to the homeless.

COA Groups

A number of people have documented the positive results experienced by COAs when they participate in groups that focus on being the child of an alcoholic (Miller, 1983;[14] Hawley, 1981;[15] Deckman, 1982; [16] Peitler, 1980; [17] Hughes, 1977; [18] Fairchild, 1974; [19] Weir, 1970 [20]). DiCicco et al. also documented the positive results for adolescent children of alcoholics when they participated in integrated groups that provided general alcohol education. [21]

Groups can be a particularly strong modality for working with COAs. By participating in a group with other COAs, individuals will experience the following benefits:

- Reduced Isolation
- New Ways of Coping
- Positive Peer Support

- Practice Sharing Feelings
- Confrontation When Needed
- Increased Readiness for Alateen [22]

The Goals for COA groups include:

To reduce isolation
To practice identifying and expressing feelings
To increase understanding of the parents
To learn coping strategies

Regardless of the duration of the group, all groups should include education about parental alcoholism and how it affects children. The group should begin with an educational style since the classroom is often the only group a COA feels safe in because the roles and rules are consistent and clearly defined.

Several manuals for leading COA groups for elementary and middle school aged children are available.

Sexual Abuse and Other Forms of Child Abuse

All COA service providers must report child abuse to the proper authorities. It is critical that COAs understand the limits of confidentiality at the beginning of their participation in programs so they can choose what to self disclose. When a child reports abuse, the service provider should ask the child what he/she wants to happen, and discuss possible ways of stopping the abuse and protecting the child; such as having the family participate in court ordered counseling, having the abusing father removed from the home, having the child leave the home, etc. Ideally, COA service providers, depending how well they know the child, can report the abuse and make suggestions for how it's handled. In most states child protective workers, are overloaded, undertrained, and undersupervised. As a result, many appreciate suggestions and will incorporate them into their handling of the case. Service providers who report child abuse should be prepared for the child's anger and sense of betrayal. They should explain to the child why he or she is making the report and continue to provide ongoing help for the child.

Often COA service providers are reluctant to report some child abuse because the child abuse/protection system in most states is less than ideal and there is a fear that reporting will do more harm then good. While this may be true, all cases must be reported because the consequence of not reporting are serious. It may help to keep in mind that a child abuse report can hurt a child. Hurt children can heal, but dead children cannot.

Service providers to COAs should go out of their way to increase the understanding of COAs by child abuse/protective workers, legal guardians, and judges.

Cultural Issues

All providers of services to COAs should be culturally sensitive. This includes knowing how children of different cultural groups will respond to similar situations and providing culturally appropriate educational materials when they are available. For example, Brisbane and Womble [23] point out that an African American COA may have more difficulty saying negative things about a parent than a caucasian COA. Professionals should also be aware of how families from different cultural backgrounds define family, view "getting help", and the dynamics that exist when the service provider is of a different cultural background than the child.

TRAINING AND QUALIFICATIONS

The training and qualifications of providers of services to COAs vary depending on the range of services being provided. The person creating a bulletin board display of government posters for COAs obviously does not need the same qualifications as some-one who is doing therapy with COAs. However, in viewing the continuum of services for COAs once the service provider goes past awareness, the qualifications necessary include a minimum understanding of child and adolescent development, knowledge of techniques for working with the child at different developmental stages and emotional states, and knowledge of alcoholism and drug abuse.

Until recently, most child specialists did not have alcoholism knowledge and most alcoholism professionals didn't have child development knowledge and skills in working with children of different ages. To understand a "blackout", but not be able to explain it to a child so it can be understood, will not help COAs just as to be an expert in working with children but not know what a blackout is will not be helpful.

The ability to be objective in working with COAs is critical. Adult COAs should be sure to have worked through their own issues and be aware and get help if they re-emerge. For example, an untreated adult COA may try to cap a young COA's expression of angry or hurt feelings because they access feelings and memories of the counselor's childhood that the counselor that have been repressed or sublimated and the counselor doesn't want to deal with them. On the other extreme, a child may begin discussing an experience that was similar to the counselor's childhood experience. The counselor may assume that the child's feelings about the experience are the same as the counselor's past feelings and not give the child the opportunity to discuss it further, and then misread the situation and the child's feelings. Professional supervision is extremely useful in determining if these situations are occurring.

Professional supervision is also useful in determining the appropriateness and timing of self-disclosure. Most professionals working with COAs are asked if they grew up in an alcoholic home. The general rules of professional self disclosure to a client/patient apply. Self disclosure should only occur if it's in the child's best interest. If counselors disclose they are COAs too early in the relationship, the child might assume the counselor automatically understands and not make the effort to organize and express his/her own experience. If counselors who are not COAs share this with the child too early, the child might wonder, "how can she/he possibly understand and help me?". The child might also be too embarrassed about his/her experience and feelings.

On the other hand, self-disclosure can be helpful at the end of the counseling relationship. For example, acknowledging a counselor's own situation as a COA may give a child hope for a healthy future. Acknowledging not being a COA shows COAs that others can understand and help.

Counselors who are recovering alcoholics who drank as parents should be cautioned when considering work with COAs. Hearing the rage and sadness of a young or adolescent COA can ignite feelings of guilt in the counselor who for the first time may be hearing the magnitude of the impact of parental alcoholism on children and then wonder if his/her children also felt like this. Again, having worked through these issues and receiving professional supervision are critical for the counselor.

ADOLESCENT DRINKING AND OTHER DRUG USE

Treatment

It is estimated that 80-90% of all adolescents in treatment for their own alcoholism or other drug dependency are COAs. Until very recently, their COA issues were not addressed in treatment. (It is the author's view that this was one of the reasons for the high rate of relapse in adolescents). The COA issues were not addressed because treatment professionals applied the wise practice of not dealing with a chemically dependent adult's COA issues, until a year of sobriety has been achieved, to adolescents. This practice is based on the idea that dealing with COA issues before a year of sobriety will stimulate a high degree of anxiety which could then trigger a relapse.

While this is a wise practice in treating adults, it is an inappropriate practice in treating adolescents who are emotionally dependent, and often financially dependent, on their parents. Many chemically dependent adolescents compare and contrast their chemical use to their parents, may have to attend AA, NA, or CA meetings with their parents, or may live with or return home to active parental alcoholism. They may be using chemicals as a way of coping with the parental alcoholism, and may have parents who sabotage their recovery.[24]

Prevention

While all schools are mandated to provide alcohol and drug education to students, it is ironic that COAs, the group most at risk for becoming alcoholic, may be least affected by the education. There are several explanations for this. First, many COAs do not believe the negative consequences of drinking because of conflicts with the messages at home; such as "people only die if they drink too much. I don't drink that much!" To believe that alcohol is harmful would force them to believe that the parent will die. A young child cannot live with the constant fear of abandonment and maintain emotional health. Therefore, the child decides that "the amount of alcohol my mom drinks is OK." Second, many COAs become highly anxious during alcohol and drug education and "tune out" or act out, including cutting class. They don't learn the information because they are "not there."

Third, alcohol and drug education has rarely addressed the vulnerability issues. Few COAs understand how they are more vulnerable, such as possibly having a high tolerance to alcohol, and processing alcohol in the body differently.

Alcohol and drug prevention programs must address these issues by providing developmentally appropriate COA-specific material for COAs even if they are not identified. Prevention programs using curriculums should also offer individual attention to COAs, just as schools provide "extra help" for students who have difficulty with other subjects.

CONCLUSION

Despite the growing number of COA-specific services, a continuum of services in many different settings are still needed. In providing services, the needs of the child should be matched to the level of service needed at that time. To do this, a careful assessment of the child and the impact of the parents' drinking on the child must be done.

Providers of services to COAs must maintain objectivity to be most effective and should use professional supervision to monitor if personal issues are interfering with the delivery of services.

Finally, alcohol and drug education must be more responsive to the learning styles of COAs and adolescent chemical dependency treatment programs must address COA issues if we are going to begin to break the cycle of addiction.

References

1   Booz Allen Hamilton, Inc. An Assessment of the Needs of and Resources for Children of Alcoholic Parents. Prepared for NIAAA 1974.

2   National Institute on Alcohol Abuse and Alcoholism. Services for Children of Alcoholics Research Monograph No. 4, DHHS Publ. No. ADM 81-1007. Washington, D.C., U.S. Government Printing Office, 1981.

3   Ibid., p. iii.

4   Children of Alcoholics Foundation, Directory of National Resources for Children of Alcohlics, New York, 1986.

5   Woodside, M., Henderson, B. Samuels, P. Parental Consent: Helping Children of Addicted Parents Get Help. Children of Alcoholics Foundation, Inc., NY, 1991.

6   Black, Claudia. It Will Never Happen to Me!. Denver, M.A.C., 1981.

7   Deutsch, C., Di Cicco, L., Mills, D. "Reaching Children From Families wiht Alcoholism." In: Levin, M., ed. Proceedings of the 29th Annual Meeting of the Alcohol and Drug Problems Association of North America, 1978. Washington, D.C.

8   National Institute on Alcohol Abuse and Alcoholism. Preventing Alcohol Problems Through A Student Assitance Program, DHHS Publ. No. ADM 84-1344, Washington, D.C., U.S. Government Printing Office, 1984.

9   O'Gorman, P. and Ross, R. "Children of Alcohlics in the Juvenile Justice System." Alcohol Health and Research World, Vol 8, No. 4, 1984.

10   Kohlberg, L. The Philosophy of Moral Development: Moral Stages and the Idea of Justice. San Francisco: Harper & Row, 1981.

11   Gilligan, C. In a Differrent Voice: Psychological Theory and Women's Development. Cambridge: Harvard University Press, 1982.

12   Beardslee, W. and Podorefsky, D. "Resilient Adolescents Whose Parents Have Serious Affective and Other Psychiatric Disorders: Importance of Self-Understanding and Relationships", American Journal of Psychiatry 145:1, January, 1988.

13   Morehouse, Ellen. "Working in the Schools with Children of Alcoholic Parents." Health and Social Work, Vol. 4, No. 4, 1984.

14   Miller, N. "Group Psychotherapy in a School Setting for Adolescent Children of Alcoholics". Group, Vol. 7, 1983.

15   Hawley, N.P. and Brown, C.L. "Use of Group Treatment with Children of Alcoholics". *Social Casework*, Vol. 62, No. 1, 1981.

16   Deckman, J. and Downs, B. "A Group Treatment Approach for Adolescent Children of Alcoholic Parents." *Social Work Groups* Vol. 5, 1982.

17   Peitler, E.J. A Comparison of the effectiveness of group counseling and Alateen on the psychological adjustment of two groups of adolescent sons of alcoholic fathers. Ph.D. dissertation, St. John's University, 1980.

18   Hughes, J.M. "Adolescent Children of Alcoholic Parents and the Relationship of Alateen to These Children." *Journal of Consulting and Clinical Psychology*, Vol. 49, 1977.

19   Fairchild, D.M. "Teen Group I.: A Pilot Project in Group Therapy with Adolescent CHildren of Alcoholic Patients." *Journal of the Ft. Logan Mental Health Center*, Vol. 2, 1964.

20   Weir, W.R. "Conseling Youth Whose Parents Are Alcoholic: A Means to an End as well as an End in Itself." *Journal of Alcohol Education*, 16, 1970.

21   Di Cicco, L. Davis, R., Hogan J., MacLean, A. and Orenstein, A. "Group Experiences for Children of Alcoholics." *Alcohol Health and Research World*, Vol. 8, No. 4, 1984.

22   Morehouse, E. In: Ackerman, R., ed. *Growing in the Shadow*, Pompano Beach, Fla. : Health Communications, 1986.

23   Brisbane, F. and Womble, M. *A Model for Working with Black Children of Alcoholic and Drug Addicted Parents*. The National Black Alcoholism Council, 1987.

24   Morehouse, E. "Working with Alcohol-Abusing Children of Alcoholics". *Alcohol Health and Research World*, Vol. 8, No. 4, 1984.

MORALITY IN COAs: Revisiting the Syndrome of Over-Responsibility

Sybil Wolin Ph.D.
Steven Wolin M.D.

Introduction

As a clinician, you are undoubtedly familiar with the clinical portrait of the overly responsible child of an alcoholic (4, 8, 22). The syndrome has been widely described; you have probably seen more than a few clients who fit the diagnosis. Variously called hypermature, co-dependent, responsible ones, or enablers, overly responsible children take charge when alcoholic parents abdicate their roles. These children respond to their parents' drinking by growing up fast. They react to the early signs of a parent's drunken rampage by putting pajamas on the younger kids and taking them to a neighbor's house to sleep. They do the weekly marketing and cook meals. They take care of the family's laundry. They clean the house and throw away their parents' broken liquor bottles. And they go out late at night to bring dad or mom home from the bar.

As a result of these children's efforts, some structure and consistency are achieved at home. However, according to conventional wisdom, the price they pay is great, amounting to no less than giving up significant parts of their youths. Often, as they grow into adulthood, overly responsible children become anxious, depressed, tense, and distant from others. They may enter into unhealthy relationships and overwork themselves to the point of exhaustion. Or attempting desperately to compensate for the lost pleasures of childhood, they may become excessively demanding and dependent. In all, overly responsible children bear the scars of their past.

We suggest that the pessimistic picture of overly responsible COAs, drawn above, is a partial truth which reflects a clinical bias toward identifying pathology in COAs. Having worked under the influence of a pathology bias, we know well that there are good reasons for it. Talking about pathology feels safe to clinicians; talking about strengths feels dangerous.

First, talking about deficits and symptoms gives us a professional legitimacy that talking about strengths does not. Second, our vocabulary of strengths is scant and pallid in contrast to the technical, high sounding lexicon available to us for discussing pathology. Third, the topic of strengths is difficult emotionally. Turning our attention away from forces that are harmful and dangerous to children violates our natural sympathies toward the young. To add to the matter, talking about their strengths instead can feel like excusing the inexcusable. Fourth, the topic feels politically risky. We are rightfully wary that professional acknowledgement of strengths in children of hardship could easily become justification for trimming the budget by withdrawing support services.

For all of these reasons, a bias toward pathology is understandable. Nonetheless, it is also limiting and warrants our scrutiny. Emphasizing, as it does, problems and symptoms, a pathology bias diverts the clinician's interest away from clients' strengths. It can lull us into using such negatively tinged descriptors as "overly responsible," "co-dependent," and "enabler," and ultimately it leaves us with little to build on in therapy. Therefore, in this chapter, we invite you to examine the pathology bias by focusing on the usefulness of "over-responsibility" as a diagnosis and as a therapeutic term to be used with clients.

MORALITY vs. DEFENSIVENESS

The motivation of COAs who step into the roles abdicated by their parents has been typically attributed to the chaotic atmosphere that prevails in homes overrun by alcohol (1). This connection between the COAs' behavior and their disrupted home lives makes good sense and rests on well accepted precepts emerging from the field of child development.

We know that children need and want stability and structure. Families disrupted by the influence of alcohol, all too often, provide neither. Lacking basics such as food, clothing, safety and medical care, COAs learn that the adults around them cannot be counted on to provide. Consequently, many COAs act defensively to establish, by themselves, the structure that they and the rest of the family require.

Given the range of choices that are easier and perhaps more likely and natural for adolescents, we are struck by the widespread acceptance of a diagnostic formulation which reduces taking over for an absent parent to a defense. Alternately, we suggest that such a choice can more accurately be seen as a moral achievement which, like any other achievement, comes at a price.

It does not seem farfetched to us that a strong sense of compassion, fairness, and decency, each of which we include in our concept of morality, account for bringing mom or dad home from the bar rather than letting either one be put out on the street at closing time. Nor does it seem hard to imagine that moral sentiments could prompt COAs into taking care of the younger kids in their families despite the personal costs. What does seem strange to us is that the moral sensibilities and the strength of character of many COAs can escape clinical attention, be misconstrued or even disparaged as pathology, or be spoken about primarily in terms of psychological costs.

A relevant perspective can be found in the work of Robert Coles, the noted child psychologist (4). Coles, has traveled around the world to interview children living in dire conditions. He wanted to know what course child development takes in environments commonly thought to bring out the worst in people.

Coles' work has taken him and his wife Jane to the American ghettos and migrant camps, the Brazilian favelas, and the South African mandated homelands. Where corruption and brutality are rampant, Coles found children who could judge right from wrong and who were honest, charitable, and fair. Coles marveled because there was little in the environment of these children which could account for their development.

Though Coles had been psychoanalytically trained, he did not even hint at a defensive component to the morality he observed among downtrodden children. Instead, he sees their morality as a positive, sustaining force that gives purpose and direction to their lives. Morality, according to Coles, is not an antidote to pain, nor does it prevent pain. Rather, morality is an accomplishment that makes life possible despite pain. We suggest that concept of morality, as described by Coles, has untapped value for organizing our clinical thinking and work with COAs. Consider the case of Terry and the injustice we would do her by diminishing the role of moral values in the choices she made.

TERRY - A CASE STUDY

Terry is a young woman in her twenties whom we interviewed for our video series "Survivor's Pride: Building Resilience in Youth at Risk" (11). By her own description, Terry played the role of mother in her family, meeting all the household and child care obligations that her alcoholic parents neglected.

Terry's earliest memory of her parents' drinking and her own abandonment dates back to kindergarten. The eldest of four children, she assumed more and more of the care of her young brothers and sisters throughout her elementary school years. By high school, she was totally in charge of the household, and while she was determined to go away to college, and did go, separation from her family was a wrench. In her freshman year, when Terry's parents divorced, her mother left the home. The three younger children remained in the care of their father. Worried about their physical safety as well as their emotional well being, Terry interrupted her college career for two-and-a-half years to come home and hold the family together.

Terry told us that by choosing to return home, she was following the dictates of her conscience. She said further, that to this day, she felt good about what she had done. Nonetheless, she suffered. Being at home when she wanted to be in college was painful, and she began to drink.

At the time we interviewed Terry, she had not been drinking for over three years. She had some expectable symptoms related to her childhood, namely perfectionism, a recurrent feeling that she "could always do more," and some difficulty "playing." There was also a good deal that was positive in Terry's life. She was engaged to be married, had thought carefully and constructively about the nature of her relationship with her fiance, and could share her feelings with him freely. As she described it, they were "good friends."

Terry was also gratified to be completing an undergraduate degree in elementary education. She saw her career choice as a carryover from her past success with young children, both as a baby sitter and as an older sister. She said, "I love working with kids. A lot of my jobs were with kids... and I took care of my younger brother and sisters ... They thought I was their mother ... I babysat all over the neighborhood. Not just on my block because parents would refer me to other parents, and I'd get calls all the time. I was booked months in advance. And those families still remember me and ask about me."

In addition to extending her early loving experiences with children, teaching offered Terry an arena for exercising her moral commitment. She saw in education the opportunity to have the same positive influence that her own teachers had on her. She said, "I've always wanted to be a teacher, and even more so now, realizing that I can make a difference , not only in academic education. I had some really kind supporting teachers I remember, and they definitely helped me."

Shortly before we interviewed Terry, she had seen her mother. She related the incident to us. Having recently achieved sobriety, Terry's mother wanted to repair relationships with her children. She contacted Terry with the intended goal of making amends. Accordingly, she acknowledged all the "terrible things" Terry was forced to do as a child. She then apologized and asked for Terry's forgiveness.

For Terry's mother, the apology had the likely effect of relieving guilt. For Terry, however, it hurt more than it helped, running afoul of her view of her self as a caring, decent, and competent person. Moreover, the apology robbed Terry of the pride she felt in her behavior as a child, and it undercut her efforts to rest her current decisions on her past accomplishments.

Terry explained, "Pride ... hum ... I get a lot of the opposite from my mom. She's always apologizing now that she's in recovery.

And she feels that she made me responsible for so many things, and it's hard to be proud when she's saying that this was such a horrible thing. So it's kind of a dilemma for me cause I am proud. I did the right thing and I feel like I did a good job sometimes, the best I could, more than would be expected of a child. Then to have her tell me that she is so sorry and it was horrible and that's not the way it should have been. She's right, but ... how about a pat on the back?"

THE DAMAGE MODEL

For clinicians to view Terry with a pathology bias, to dwell primarily on the psychological costs of her choices, to label her as overly responsible is to make the same error in judgement that her mother made. We call the mindset that spawns such pessimistic pathology-oriented thinking the Damage Model (10).

In the Damage Model (pictured below) troubled families, such as those with alcoholism, are seen as toxic agents, and offspring are regarded as victims of their parents' harmful actions.

COAs, according to the Damage Model, are vulnerable, and locked into the family. The best they can do is cope or contain the family's harmful influence at considerable cost to themselves. Inevitably, the accumulating price of coping takes its toll and results in symptoms and behaviors that make up the general category of pathologies. In adolescence and adulthood, pathologies are layered on pathologies, and eventually the child is no better off than his or her troubled parent.

The role of the therapist in this scenario is to uncover and give voice to the hurt feelings and anger in COAs such as Terry. Therapy aims to promote healing through the processes of grieving and of expressing hurt and anger. Biased toward disease and fixing what's wrong with the client, the Damage Model accommodates neither Terry's positive valuation of her own actions nor her resources to help herself. A different approach is required to understand Terry and others like her more fully.

THE CHALLENGE MODEL

© Drs. Steven & Sybil Wolin
Project Resilience
Washington, D.C.

PATHOLOGIES

RESILIENCIES

THE CHALLENGE MODEL

The Challenge Model (pictured below) builds on the Damage Model (10). We intend it as an amplification or complement to the Damage Model and not as a refutation or replacement.

The Challenge Model starts, like the Damage Model, with the observation that troubled families can inflict considerable harm on their children. In the Challenge Model, however, two forces, represented by interlocking arrows, are at work as the child and the family interact. The troubled family is seen as a danger to the child, as it is in the Damage Model, and also as an opportunity. Children are vulnerable to their parents' harm, but they are also challenged to rebound by becoming active agents in their own lives. As a result of the interplay between damage and challenge, the children in troubled families are left with pathologies that do not disappear completely and resiliencies that limit the influence of their damage and promote their growth and well-being. The shaded and unshaded areas on the Challenge Model diagram represent the contrasting elements of strength and weakness in the inner life and outward behavior of COAs like Terry.

In the process of developing the Challenge Model, we interviewed adult children of troubled families, including children from alcoholic families. Our aim was to uncover both the strengths and the damage that resulted from their early, difficult experiences. Our analysis of the interview transcripts certainly revealed elements of pathology. But, unconstrained by a primary interest in sickness, we could also see common positive themes or clusters of strengths. We have called these clusters of strength resiliencies and have named them as follows: insight, independence, relationships, initiative, creativity, humor and morality. For the purposes of this paper, we will focus exclusively on morality.

THE DEVELOPMENTAL UNFOLDING OF MORALITY

We define morality as the activity of an informed conscience (10). It is the wish for a good personal life grown large and inclusive. In adults, morality is defined as "serving" or devoting time and energy to improving institutions, community and the world. For example, choosing a career in teaching, as Terry did, because of the opportunity it offers for helping children; including charitable

THE DAMAGE MODEL

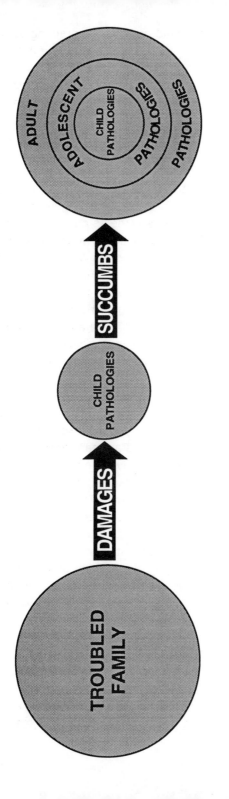

contributions in one's household budget; volunteering to tutor the illiterate; donating blood to a blood bank; supporting political reform; looking out for friends who are alone at holiday time; giving up a favorite activity to help a sick friend; reducing a standard fee for a needy client; writing a letter to the editor about biased reporting; or helping a mother search for a lost child on the beach. Morality is the capacity to move beyond self interest and act on the basis of a larger common good.

As the generous spirit of the people we interviewed revealed itself in these and other examples, we were deeply touched. We also wondered how those, given so little as children, had honed their moral sensibilities. Their explanations, which were similar, did not reflect an inclination to see themselves "as over-responsible" but rather as spiritual, mindful, generous, and moral people. For example, Noreen, an adult child of an alcoholic, said, "coming from the kind of home life I had . . . I'm left with a deep awareness of just how fragile the good things in life are and how easily they could disappear or just not be ... I have an abiding of appreciation for what I have -- a sense of indebtedness and an obligation to repay."

Almost uniformly, the kind of sentiment expressed here could be traced back through early childhood and adolescence. Noreen, for example, said, "I knew my father was a mean machine. I didn't think that I or anyone else in the family deserved his violence. My father's brutality was his problem. In fact, that was one of the worst parts about growing up in my family. There was no rhyme or reason to him. What he did was so unconnected to what we did."

Noreen's words strongly suggest that, from a young age, she was capable of accurately judging the injustice of her parent's behavior. We suggest that, as children, many COAs had the same good judgement as Noreen. Indeed, applying a right - wrong standard to their parents was the first step in the achievement of their morality.

In keeping with a Damage Model, COAs are not normally credited with the early achievement of morality. Instead, the view has prevailed that young children are emotionally incapable of judging the rights and wrongs of their parents' behavior (2, 6, 7). Wanting and needing good parents in order to be safe in an overwhelming world, they are blinded to their parents' faults. Even when parents are abusive and neglectful, children will not hold them to account. Instead, they will blame themselves and construe the abuse and neglect as treatment they deserve. In short, on the basis of a pathology bias, abuse specialists (8) have become convinced that children will make themselves "bad" in order to preserve an image of their parents as "good."

More in keeping with the Challenge Model, our interviews revealed a **shifting** moral awareness among COAs, as children, rather than a **stable** sense of themselves as bad and their parents as good. At their neediest times, they succumbed and were, in fact, willing to accept the blame for their own abuse and neglect. At other times, however, they were able to be strong, to brave the world alone, and to see matters more clearly. They knew that abuse was bad and that they deserved better.

The research of Dr. Robert L. Selman confirms our impression (9). In a study looking at social development, Selman showed that young children **are** capable of acknowledging that parents are fallible. Asked hypothetical questions, seven-year-olds differentiated between the justifiable actions and the mistakes of their parents. In their opinion, punishment is not necessarily deserved because a parent metes it out. Rather, punishment can be warranted or unwarranted, fair or unfair. The seven-year-olds who spoke to Selman were capable, as the Challenge Model suggests, of skepticism toward parents, saying that it is wrong to punish children without considering the reasons for their behaviors.

In adolescence, the capacity for judging, found in our interviews and confirmed by Selman's research, develops into a coherent system of values, including decency, honesty, fairness, and justice. We suggest that this value system drives the behavioral pattern we have tagged as "over-responsibility." As Noreen told us, "It was a matter of tolerance. I saw all the suffering and I couldn't abide it. The worst was that my father would go after the younger kids, the little ones who couldn't defend themselves. I felt that I had to protect the little ones. It was a moral obligation, something I couldn't avoid, something any decent person would do."

CONCLUSION

In this paper, we have shown that the behavior of COAs who meet the obligations neglected by alcoholic parents has been seen commonly as a defense. As such, this behavior pattern is believed to serve an adaptive purpose for COAs when they are young but, ultimately, it becomes the foundation for pathology in adulthood. Alternatively, we have proposed that the COAs' evolving moral sensibilities underlie the willingness and capacity to step in for neglectful and/or abusive alcoholic parents. Therefore, their behavior, which has been commonly tagged as "overly responsible," would be more properly regarded as an achievement with a price rather than as a defense.

NOTES

1. Black C: *Children of Alcoholics as Youngsters-Adolescents-Adults."It Will Never Happen to Me"*. New York, Ballantine Books, 1981

2. Bowlby J: On knowing what you're not supposed to know and feeling what you're not supposed to feel. *Canadian Journal of Psychiatry* 24: 403-408, 1979

3. Cermak TL: *The Road to Recovery. A Time to Heal*. Los Angeles, California, Jeremy P. Tarcher, Inc., 1976

4. Coles R: *The Moral Life of Children*. Boston, Houghton Mifflin, 1986

5. Friel J, Friel L: Adult Children. *The Secrets of Dysfunctional Families*. Pompano Beach, Florida, Health Communications, Inc., 1988

6. Kohlberg, L: *The Philosophy of Moral Development*. Volume I. San Francisco, Harper & Row, 1981

7. Miller, A: *The Drama of the Gifted Child*. New York, Basic Books, 1981

8. Rieker, PR & Carmen, E: The victim-to-patient process: The disconfirmation and transformation of abuse. *American Journal of Orthopsychiatry* 56: 360-370, 1986

9. Selman, R: *The Growth of Interpersonal Understanding: Developmental and Clinical Analyses*. New York, Academic Press, 1980

10. Wolin, SJ & Wolin S: *The Resilient Self. How Survivors of Troubled Families Rise Above Adversity*. New York, Villard Books, 1993

11. *Survivor's Pride. Building Resilience in Youth at Risk*. Verona, Wisconsin, Attainment Co., 1993